short

you

this year!

God bless you ♡

Love, Mom + Dad

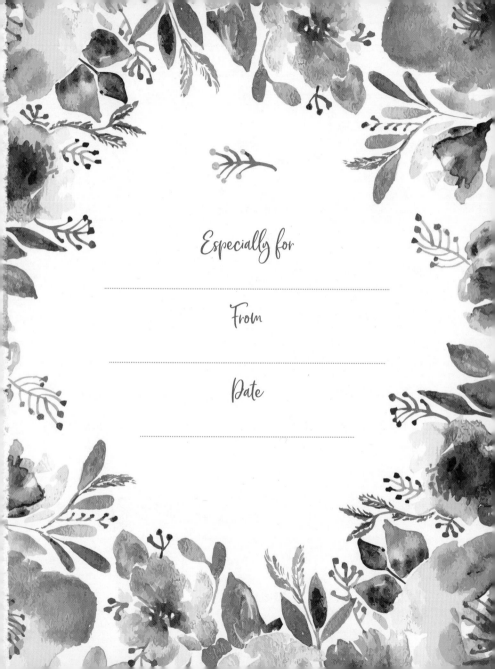

Especially for

...............................................................

From

...............................................................

Date

...............................................................

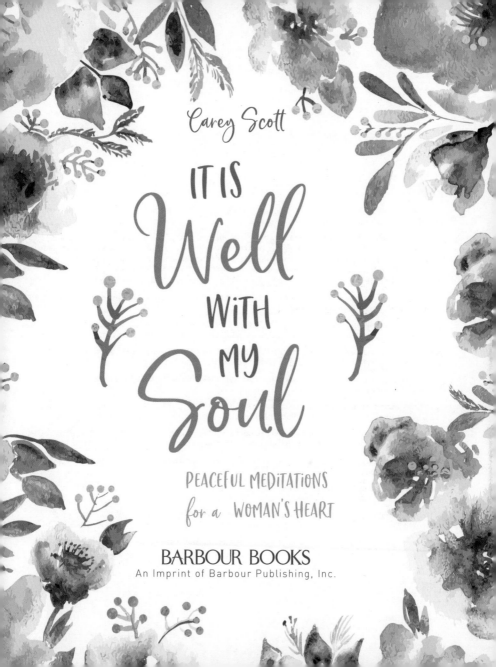

Carey Scott

# IT IS
# Well
## WITH
## MY
# Soul

PEACEFUL MEDITATIONS
*for a* WOMAN'S HEART

## BARBOUR BOOKS
An Imprint of Barbour Publishing, Inc.

*Our mission is to inspire the world with the life-changing message of the Bible.*

 Member of the
Evangelical Christian
Publishers Association

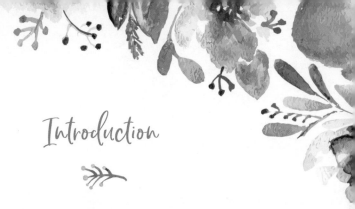

# Introduction

Every day we're bombarded with situations and circumstances that threaten to pull us from the peace of Jesus. From struggles in our relationships to fear for our future to tough seasons of life, maintaining a harmonious heart is a battle. We often forget who we are in Jesus and fall into old patterns of living that cause uneasiness. Rather than trust God with our mess, we cling to control and try to fix things ourselves. Instead of activating faith, we obsess over details, certain of horrible outcomes. And when we allow our hearts to stay stirred up in anxiety and worry, we feel hopeless.

But friend, life doesn't have to be this way. You don't have to figure things out on your own, desperate for calmer times. When you invite God into your anxious heart, you will find calm in the middle of chaos. You'll experience a peace that makes no sense to the world. And regardless of the struggles that will come your way, with the Lord's help you will be able to say, *It is well with my soul.*

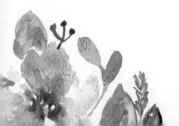

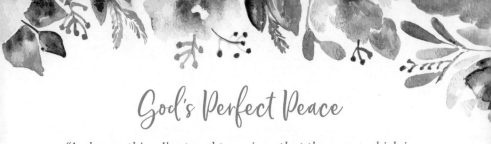

# God's Perfect Peace

*"And everything I've taught you is so that the peace which is in me will be in you and will give you great confidence as you rest in me. For in this unbelieving world you will experience trouble and sorrows, but you must be courageous, for I have conquered the world!"*

JOHN 16:33 TPT

Sometimes peace eludes us. There's no shortage of people and situations that threaten to pull us out of the comfort we have in God's perfect peace. We battle fear and insecurities because we allow ourselves to focus on the what-ifs and if-onlys. Every day requires us to make a deliberate decision to ask God to fill our hearts with His peace so we can thrive in our tasks and responsibilities.

* * * * * * * * * * * * * * * * * * * * * * * * * * * * * * * *

*Father, I need Your help. Today I am battling things that make me feel scared and ineffective. I want to be a strong and confident woman, and I simply cannot do that if I'm not surrounded by Your perfect peace. Will You please give that to me? In Jesus' name I pray. Amen.*

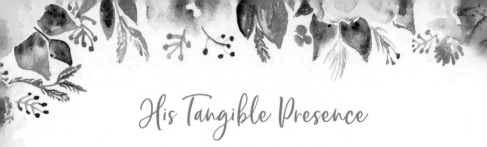

# His Tangible Presence

*Now, may the Lord himself, the Lord of peace, pour into
you his peace in every circumstance and in every possible way.
The Lord's tangible presence be with you all.*

2 Thessalonians 3:16 tpt

Do you ever feel lonely? It's different from being alone. Some of us are more introverted, so we need that space to regroup. Others may be more extroverted—loving to be surrounded by people—but can still appreciate solitude from time to time. But being lonely is a different beast altogether. It often creates a deep longing to be seen and noticed and leaves one feeling unloved.

God will always be a constant companion. You may feel alone, but you're not alone. Why not ask Him to replace that empty feeling with His tangible presence?

. . . . . . . . . . . . . . . . . . . . . . . . . . . . . . . . . . . . . . . . . .

*Father, today I feel lonely. Thank You that You're always with me,
no matter what. It does my heart good to know that You'll never
walk away from me. Will You please let me feel Your tangible presence
right now? I need to know You're here. In Jesus' name I pray. Amen.*

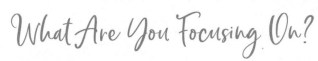

# What Are You Focusing On?

*"You will keep in perfect and constant peace the one whose mind is steadfast [that is, committed and focused on You— in both inclination and character], because he trusts and takes refuge in You [with hope and confident expectation]."*
ISAIAH 26:3 AMP

When you're struggling with something, where's your focus? Do you tend to give all your attention to the problem, replaying the event over and over in your mind? Do you come up with a list of responses you wish you'd said and practice saying them in case it happens again? Is the issue the main topic of conversation with your friends? Do you ruminate about it with a family member? Or do you take it right to the Lord, asking for His help? Maybe you need wisdom and discernment, strength and perseverance, or courage and confidence. Next time, choose to keep your focus on God and let Him be the source of what you need.

. . . . . . . . . . . . . . . . . . . . . . . . . . . . . . . . . .

*Father, help me focus on You when I'm struggling. Help me trust You with my problems. In Jesus' name I pray. Amen.*

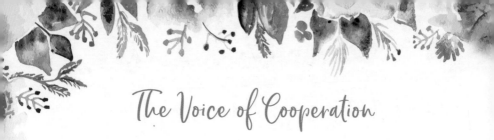

# The Voice of Cooperation

*"You're blessed when you can show people how to cooperate
instead of compete or fight. That's when you discover who
you really are, and your place in God's family."*
MATTHEW 5:9 MSG

We live in a world where people are so quick to be offended. And these offenses can keep us from working together for the common good. Instead of combining forces, we take sides and point fingers. Even if others have good ideas or solid plans, many won't consider working as a team because we are so divided. It's a sad state, really.

With God's help though, you can be a voice for cooperation. Your voice can be influential when infused by the Lord. Your words are powerful when spoken in His authority. And you can be a uniting force by simply allowing God to use you for kingdom work.

* * * * * * * * * * * * * * * * * * * * * * * * * * * * * * * * * * * *

*Father, I want to be a peacemaker and a peacekeeper, and I'm willing
to be the voice of cooperation. Give me the confidence and courage to
do the work You set before me. In Jesus' name I pray. Amen.*

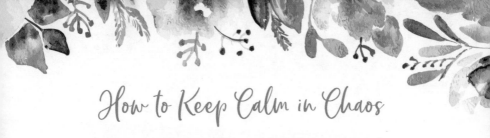

# How to Keep Calm in Chaos

*Don't be anxious about things; instead, pray. Pray about
everything. He longs to hear your requests, so talk to God
about your needs and be thankful for what has come.*

PHILIPPIANS 4:6 VOICE

How are you supposed to stay calm when life's storms rock your world?
How can you keep from worrying when your marriage, finances, family,
health, career, or kids are falling apart? Sometimes this command feels
too big, and we disqualify ourselves because we simply cannot envision
living anxiety-free in today's world. But you absolutely can stay in calm
head and heart spaces—even when chaos surrounds—by praying.

When you pray, you're taking the stresses of the day off your weary
shoulders and placing them at the feet of Jesus. And He offers to carry
those burdens in exchange for peace and rest. It's a win-win of epic
proportions.

* * * * * * * * * * * * * * * * * * * * * * * * * * * * * * * * *

*Father, my burdens are Yours. I cannot carry them anymore.
Please give me peace and comfort so I can thrive no matter
what comes my way. In Jesus' name I pray. Amen.*

# Make Friends, Not Enemies

*Do your best to live as everybody's friend.*
ROMANS 12:18 TPT

Being someone's friend doesn't mean you agree with everything she does or says. It doesn't mean you have to make time in your already packed schedule for coffee or lunch. You don't have to log hours on the phone or exchange birthday gifts. It doesn't imply that you have to invite each other to dinner parties or birthday parties. And your kids don't have to be besties with hers. This verse is a plea for peace.

Whenever you can, choose harmonious living. Be ready to reconcile differences. Live as a goodwill ambassador to your community of friends and family. Choose not to be easily offended, or unconcerned about upsetting others. Be generous with your kindness. Don't pick fights, engage in gossip, or assume the worst of others. Decide that whenever possible, you will walk the high road.

* * * * * * * * * * * * * * * * * * * * * * * * * * * * * * * * * * * * * *

*Father, help me choose to live in peace with everyone around me. I want to be a woman who loves You and others fiercely. In Jesus' name I pray. Amen.*

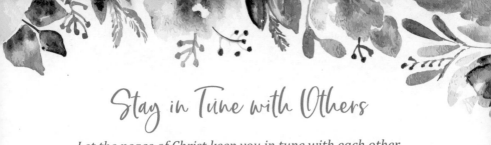

# Stay in Tune with Others

*Let the peace of Christ keep you in tune with each other,*
*in step with each other. None of this going off and*
*doing your own thing. And cultivate thankfulness.*
Colossians 3:15 msg

Have you ever heard someone sing off-key? It's almost jolting. What's more, it can throw the other singers off as they try to stay in tune. To perform well, each vocalist needs to have practiced enough and be prepared enough to be a positive contributor. This combination creates a power-packed togetherness.

Where are you off-key with others right now? Where is there angst or bad feelings brewing? What hard conversations do you need to start? Who needs to hear your apology? What is your next right step to finding harmony again?

. . . . . . . . . . . . . . . . . . . . . . . . . . . . . . . . . . . . . . . .

*Father, community can be hard to navigate. It takes time and*
*hard work to nurture those kinds of connections well. Would You*
*give me the confidence to stand up for them, refusing to settle*
*for unhealthy relationships? In Jesus' name I pray. Amen.*

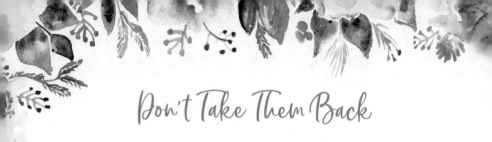

# Don't Take Them Back

*Pour out all your worries and stress upon him and leave
them there, for he always tenderly cares for you.*

1 PETER 5:7 TPT

Think of times you opened up to God and shared the deepest parts
of your heart. Maybe you were honest about fears for the future and
concerns for the present. You told Him about tough situations. You
talked about relationships stirring you up and people hurting your
feelings. You were an open book. Do you remember how good that felt
and the freedom that came with it?

Can you also remember times you tried to take burdens back so
you could be in control again? How would life be more peaceful if you
chose to leave your stresses with God, letting Him handle everything?
What if you started today?

*Father, I don't want the stress of my life anymore. I need Your
help to find peace and keep it. I'm grateful You love me
enough to carry my burdens. You're such a loving and
caring God! In Jesus' name I pray. Amen.*

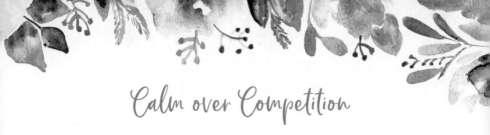

# Calm over Competition

*In every relationship be swift to choose peace
over competition, and run swiftly toward holiness,
for those who are not holy will not see the Lord.*

<small>HEBREWS 12:14 TPT</small>

Are you competitive? Do you love games because they awaken the beast within? Do you find yourself competing to see who loses the most weight, who cooks the yummiest meat loaf, whose kids make the best grades, whose husband is the most attentive, who makes the most money, who gets more party invites, and the like? Is life one big competition? Be careful, friend.

While living spirited can be fun, it can also add stress to relationships, especially when others don't look at life the same way. Make sure you're not competing because it's connected to your self-worth. Be willing to cheer on others—it's a great way to love them well.

. . . . . . . . . . . . . . . . . . . . . . . . . . . . . . . . . . . . .

*Father, sometimes I need the win to feel good about myself. . .
and I don't like that. It's not sustainable, and it puts undue strain
on my relationships. Will You help me choose calm over
competition? In Jesus' name I pray. Amen.*

# Uncontainable Joy and Perfect Peace

*Now may God, the inspiration and fountain of hope, fill you to overflowing with uncontainable joy and perfect peace as you trust in him. And may the power of the Holy Spirit continually surround your life with his super-abundance until you radiate with hope!*

ROMANS 15:13 TPT

Wouldn't it be awesome if you could have joy that overflows and complete peace on a regular basis? If God's Word says it's possible, then what keeps you from it?

Is it a screaming toddler, grief from a miscarriage, or a tough season of marriage? Is it financial stress or a scary diagnosis? Are you holding on to unforgiveness or struggling with insecurities? There's no doubt these can make you feel hopeless, but God says trusting Him through these moments will let joy and peace overflow anyway. Why not give it a try?

* * * * * * * * * * * * * * * * * * * * * * * * * * * * * * * * * * * *

*Father, please give me courage to trust You so I can have hope! There are many reasons to be filled with fear and stress, but I don't want to live that way. In Jesus' name I pray. Amen.*

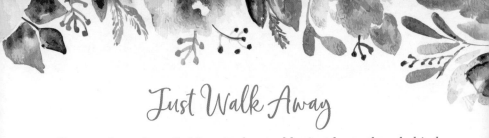

# Just Walk Away

*Walk away from the evil things in the world—just leave them behind,*
*and do what is right, and always seek peace and pursue it.*

1 PETER 3:11 VOICE

This verse is a bold plea for you to live your life in such a way that others want to follow you. It's a call to be a leader. Every day, you get to choose whether your words and actions inspire those around you.

It's easy to embrace what the world has to offer. Through movies, TV shows, advertising campaigns, magazines, the latest fashions, and social media feeds, you're bombarded daily with worldly ideals. And more times than not, their morality is miles apart from God's hope for you. What if you decided to do what is right instead of what is popular?

. . . . . . . . . . . . . . . . . . . . . . . . . . . . . . . . . . . . . . .

*Father, I want my life to reflect You. It may be easier to*
*follow the world, but I want to choose Your way instead.*
*Would You help me be bold enough to walk away from things*
*that threaten to trip me up? In Jesus' name I pray. Amen.*

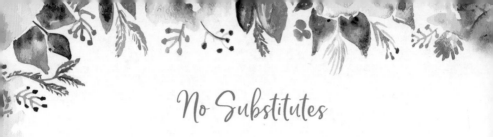

# No Substitutes

*I will lie down and fall asleep in peace because*
*you alone, LORD, let me live in safety.*
PSALM 4:8 CEB

What do you do to feel safe? Keep your doors locked, carry around pepper spray, know martial arts, or have a security system in place? And who makes you feel safe? A boyfriend or husband, a parent or roommate, a security guard at work or school? All of these can be helpful to protect you, but they're not impenetrable.

Only God can truly save. He trumps them all. The psalmist painted a powerful image of trusting the Lord to protect him, so much so that he's peaceful enough to fall asleep! How many times has sleep eluded you because you felt unsafe? Ask God to hedge you in with His protection so you can rest in His peace.

*Father, I want Your peace to still my anxious heart. I want*
*You to settle my spirit with peace. I want to find rest in You*
*above anything or anyone else. In Jesus' name I pray. Amen.*

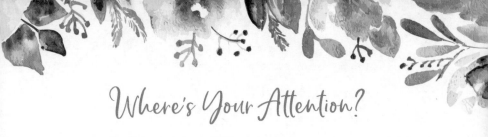

# Where's Your Attention?

*A mind focused on the flesh is doomed to death, but a mind*
*focused on the Spirit will find full life and complete peace.*
ROMANS 8:6 VOICE

Here's a hard truth: it's not about you. Are you still reading? Okay, great! Listen, friend, God made you and He doesn't make trash. You're a one-of-a-kind collection of awesomeness. But we get tripped up when we decide it really is all about us. That mind-set is selfish, and it makes us emphasize our needs above all else. It takes the spotlight off God and puts it on us instead.

The challenge comes because we have a choice. We get to decide if we focus on our own needs or if we listen for God's still, small voice telling us the next right step. This is a daily decision to be self-less and God-more, which leads to contentment.

. . . . . . . . . . . . . . . . . . . . . . . . . . . . . . . . . . . .

*Father, I confess that too often I put myself first. Help me*
*remember to focus on the Spirit because that's where*
*peace comes from. In Jesus' name I pray. Amen.*

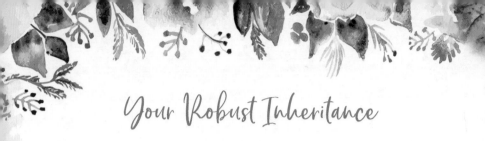

# Your Robust Inheritance

*"I leave the gift of peace with you—my peace. Not the kind of fragile peace given by the world, but my perfect peace. Don't yield to fear or be troubled in your hearts—instead, be courageous!"*

JOHN 14:27 TPT

Being a Christ follower has big benefits, one of them being a robust inheritance of peace. Why is this such a big deal? Because the peace of Jesus is hearty. It can weather storms that worldly peace can't touch. His peace will help you stand through the divorce and the diagnosis. It will allow you to maintain a worry-free heart when bankruptcy is looming or your child makes a devastating decision.

Others may not understand your calm in the chaos, your tranquility in the turmoil. But you're calm and confident because you've grabbed on to your inheritance.

. . . . . . . . . . . . . . . . . . . . . . . . . . . . . . . . . . .

*Father, please let the peace of Jesus reign in my life. Help me make wise choices to stay in that peace. And thank You for such a beautiful legacy left for me. I love You. In Jesus' name I pray. Amen.*

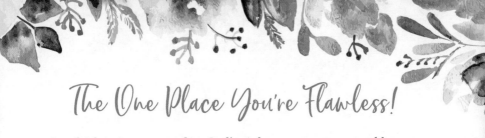

# The One Place You're Flawless!

*Our faith in Jesus transfers God's righteousness to us and he now declares us flawless in his eyes. This means we can now enjoy true and lasting peace with God, all because of what our Lord Jesus, the Anointed One, has done for us.*

ROMANS 5:1 TPT

While there's no true perfection in the world, we sure do pursue it. What's more, it's often expected of us. We waste so much time trying to be the perfect size, the perfect date, the perfect mom or wife, the perfect daughter or aunt. . .the perfect _____ (fill in the blank). We end up feeling worthless and unlovable and then try harder for acceptance. It's an endless cycle of yuck.

But friend, the only place you and the word *flawless* will be used together is when spoken by God. That's true for all of us. He looks at you through His Son and sees you as righteous. Your worldly imperfections are trumped by Jesus.

* * * * * * * * * * * * * * * * * * * * * * * * * * * * * * * * * * * * * * * *

*Father, thank You for the gift of Jesus. In His name I pray. Amen.*

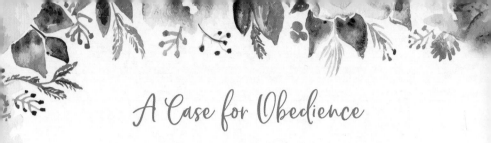

# A Case for Obedience

*The people who love your Instruction enjoy peace—*
*and lots of it. There's no stumbling for them!*
PSALM 119:165 CEB

Talk about not mincing words! The psalm gives us a straight shot of truth that leaves no room for misinterpretation. Obey God and be rewarded with peace in epic proportions. It may sound simple, but choosing to live this out every day takes grit.

There may be TV shows, movies, or book genres God asks you to give up. It may mean you say no to gatherings with people who are negative influences. You may have to step out of certain extracurricular activities. There may be relationships that aren't beneficial or helpful in your walk with the Lord that need to be revisited. But if you choose obedience, your efforts will produce a peaceful heart.

* * * * * * * * * * * * * * * * * * * * * * * * * * * * * * * * * * * * * * * *

*Father, I may not always understand what You ask of me, but I will*
*choose to obey regardless. Please open my ears and eyes so I know*
*the path You want me to walk. In Jesus' name I pray. Amen.*

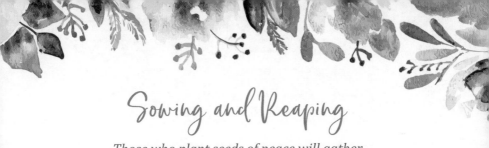

# Sowing and Reaping

*Those who plant seeds of peace will gather*
*what is right and good.*

JAMES 3:18 NLV

One of the most powerful concepts in the Bible is the connection between sowing and reaping. The idea is that the things you spend your time planting in life—kindness, generosity, righteousness, self-control, humility, peace—are the things your life will eventually produce in spades. When you choose to do the hard, intentional work on the front end, there will be a great harvest to enjoy on the other side.

What are you sowing these days? Are you living and loving well, or making wrong choices leading you away from the things of God? Are you being kind and generous with your time, talents, and treasures? Are you investing in relationships in positive ways?

*Father, I want to sow good seeds so my life will reap the benefits of my efforts. Would You help me be mindful of how I'm living? And would You change in me the things that won't produce the fruit that glorifies You? In Jesus' name I pray. Amen.*

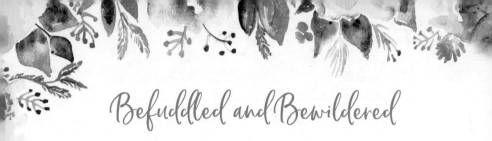

# Befuddled and Bewildered

*For God is the God of harmony, not confusion,*
*as is the pattern in all the churches of God's holy believers.*
1 CORINTHIANS 14:33 TPT

Have you ever found yourself in a situation that felt too complicated to figure out? Or in a disagreement where you struggled to follow along because it was confusing? Or listening to someone's feelings that were hard to understand? It can be so frustrating to try to navigate those befuddling and bewildering moments of life. Have you ever asked God for help?

God is not a God of confusion. So when you find yourself unable to make heads or tails of something or someone, why not ask Him for clarity of mind? Why not ask Him for discernment to see right from wrong? Why not ask Him for help? When you do, He promises to bring perspective and insight.

* * * * * * * * * * * * * * * * * * * * * * * * * * * * * * * * * * *

*Father, I don't like being confused. It makes me feel helpless.*
*Thank You for being a God of order and harmony and for being*
*willing to help me make sense of life. In Jesus' name I pray. Amen.*

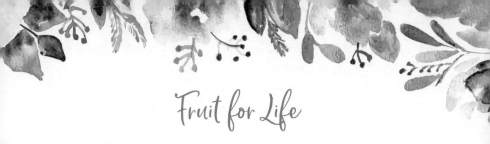

# Fruit for Life

*But the fruit produced by the Holy Spirit within you is divine love*
*in all its varied expressions: joy that overflows, peace that subdues,*
*patience that endures, kindness in action, a life full of virtue,*
*faith that prevails, gentleness of heart, and strength*
*of spirit. Never set the law above these qualities,*
*for they are meant to be limitless.*
GALATIANS 5:22–23 TPT

Because God thinks of everything, He blessed humans with gifts designed to make our lives more enjoyable for us and for those we interact with. These fruits may take time to grow to maturity, but they're accessible whenever you need to pluck them. Even better, God doesn't expect you to grow these fruits yourself. He has tasked the Holy Spirit to tend each one, perfecting them in you as you yield to His leading and teaching.

Be the kind of woman who takes full advantage of the gifts available to you through these fruits.

*Father, please grow these fruits strong in me so*
*I can live and love well. In Jesus' name I pray. Amen.*

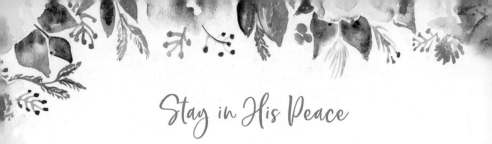

# Stay in His Peace

*Walk away from the evil things of the world,*
*and always seek peace and pursue it.*
PSALM 34:14 VOICE

The safest place for you to be is smack-dab in the middle of God's peace. When you're there, your heart isn't anxious. You aren't trying to control and manipulate everyone and everything. You're willing to trust His will and timing even when it's confusing. It may be a hard place to get to and an even harder place to hold on to, but God's peace is unmatched by anything the world has to offer.

Next time you come to a fork in the road and are faced with decisions, ask yourself, *Which choice will keep me in Jesus' peace?* Do you want the world's option, or do you want to jump onto your Father's lap and let Him calm your anxious heart?

* * * * * * * * * * * * * * * * * * * * * * * * * * * * * * * * * * * * * * * * * *

*Father, what a gift to live in Your peace. Would You give me the*
*wisdom and courage to choose it over anything the world*
*has to offer, every time. In Jesus' name I pray. Amen.*

# That Cantankerous Thought Life

*If you do this, you will experience God's peace, which is far more wonderful than the human mind can understand. His peace will keep your thoughts and your hearts quiet and at rest as you trust in Christ Jesus.*

PHILIPPIANS 4:7 TLB

Too often our thoughts end up running our lives. We allow our minds to run amok, playing out every scenario possible and eventually gravitating to horrible outcomes. And rather than living with joy and peace, we find ourselves irritable, testy, and argumentative. We don't activate our faith; we aggravate our heart.

But if we take our worries to the Lord, He promises to exchange them for His peace. Instead of following a rabbit trail to the worst-case scenario, handing our anxiety to God creates a peaceful heart. It's radical trust when we want to freak out, and it's the key to joyful living.

. . . . . . . . . . . . . . . . . . . . . . . . . . . . . . . . . . . . . . . .

*Father, I want the peace that comes from You. My life feels overwhelming and frustrating, and I'm asking You to take my worries from me in exchange for a profound sense of Your comfort. In Jesus' name I pray. Amen.*

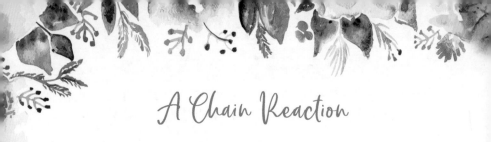

# A Chain Reaction

*When the Lord is pleased with the decisions you've made,*
*he activates grace to turn enemies into friends.*

PROVERBS 16:7 TPT

Are you anxious to calm the drama in your life? Do you often find yourself in the middle of messy situations and hurt feelings? Are you ready for smooth sailing in your relationships? Today's verse gives you the formula that makes this possible.

When you follow God's commands for living and loving well, it delights your heavenly Father. And like any proud parent, He rewards you for making the hard choices by taking those feelings of animosity between you and others and replacing them with His favor. That gracious exchange creates a sense of community and togetherness, turning rough waters into smooth sailing.

* * * * * * * * * * * * * * * * * * * * * * * * * * * * * * * * * * * * * *

*Father, You're so good to me. You are a good Daddy, and I'm thankful*
*for all the ways You choose to bless me for saying yes to Your will*
*and ways. When I have a choice, please remind me that obeying*
*You carries beautiful benefits. In Jesus' name I pray. Amen.*

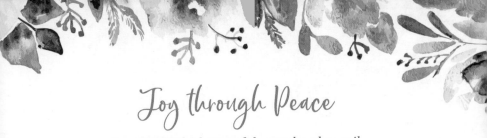

# Joy through Peace

*Deceit is in the heart of those who plan evil,
but there is joy for those who advise peace.*
PROVERBS 12:20 CEB

Whenever you have a choice, choosing peace is often the best path to take. It may sometimes seem to others that you're disengaged or uninterested. They may think you're afraid of others or unwilling to advocate for yourself. But pursuing a life filled with peace and harmony is different from raising a white flag in defeat.

It's not that you're giving up or giving in. It's that you know living offended and plotting revenge is in the opposite direction of joy. And you want joyous living for yourself and others.

Yes, there is a time to stand up for what's right. But choose carefully, because not every battle is one worth fighting.

. . . . . . . . . . . . . . . . . . . . . . . . . . . . . . . . . . . .

*Father, give me strength and wisdom to live in peace. I only have one
life here on earth, and I want to use it to glorify Your name. I can't
do that without Your peace and joy. In Jesus' name I pray. Amen.*

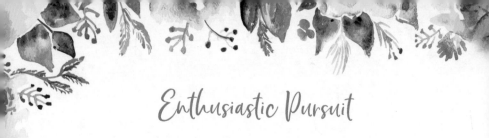

# Enthusiastic Pursuit

*So then, let us pursue [with enthusiasm] the things which*
*make for peace and the building up of one another*
*[things which lead to spiritual growth].*

ROMANS 14:19 AMP

What do you think it means to pursue with enthusiasm? How can we be excited to follow paths that lead to peace when we're deep in the middle of a mess and would rather give up than find the strength and courage to try again?

This is something we can only do with God's help. We may be eager, but life will eventually drag us down. We may have passion, but our giddyap will run dry. We may have great intentions for reconciliation, but then we get triggered in anger again.

God has to give us the ability to walk this out in real time. And He will! So, let's ask Him for enthusiastic pursuit.

. . . . . . . . . . . . . . . . . . . . . . . . . . . . . . . . . . . . .

*Father, I need Your help to make this a reality. I want to live my*
*best life. Will You help me pursue peace and encouragement*
*enthusiastically? In Jesus' name I pray. Amen.*

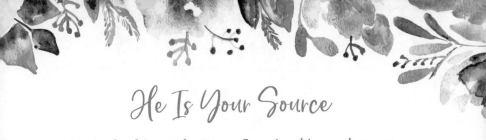

# He Is Your Source

*GOD makes his people strong. GOD gives his people peace.*
PSALM 29:11 MSG

Did you notice in today's verse that God is the One who *makes* and *gives*? These are active verbs with great intention behind them. He isn't sitting up in heaven expecting us to be the playmakers because He knows that everything good begins with Him.

Every day, God is active in your life and the world around you. He's involved in your life in ways you can't even imagine. And before He created you, He thought up plans specific to you. He decided when you'd come onto the kingdom calendar, all the details surrounding the call placed on your life, the life experiences you'd have to face, and the wisdom you'd collect from them. What's more, God equipped you with everything you need to live the life He planned.

. . . . . . . . . . . . . . . . . . . . . . . . . . . . . . . . . . . . . . . . . . .

*Father, thank You for being a God of action. I see now how You made and gave me everything I will need for this life. Knowing that gives me strength and peace. In Jesus' name I pray. Amen.*

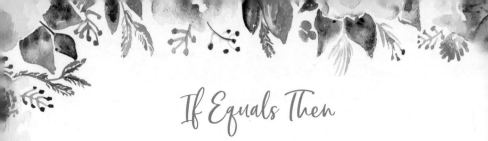

# If Equals Then

*Follow the example of all that we have imparted to you
and the God of peace will be with you in all things.*

Philippians 4:9 TPT

Paul had just finished giving the church in Philippi rules for clean living. His instructions would help them live and love well. They were teachings that reflected God's heart for them. Paul then followed with a powerful reminder that choosing this way of living would result in God's peace in their lives.

It's the concept of *if* equals *then*, and this potent notion still holds true today. Life is a series of choices that carry either blessings or consequences. Think about it in your own life. *If* you spend time in the Word, *then* you'll become closer to God. *If* you take your burdens to God, *then* you will find peace. *If* you refuse to forgive, *then* your heart will become hardened. *If* always has an outcome.

* * * * * * * * * * * * * * * * * * * * * * * * * * * * * * * * * * * * * * * * * *

*Father, I want to make good choices so I reap blessings rather than consequences. Please remind me that today's decisions affect my future. In Jesus' name I pray. Amen.*

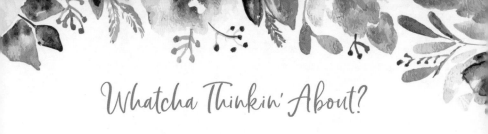

# Whatcha Thinkin' About?

*So keep your thoughts continually fixed on all that is authentic
and real, honorable and admirable, beautiful and respectful,
pure and holy, merciful and kind. And fasten your thoughts
on every glorious work of God, praising him always.*
PHILIPPIANS 4:8 TPT

This verse is a venti-sized order that can feel a bit overwhelming. It requires you to rein in those negative thoughts that often take control without you realizing it. It means you end the pity party going on in your brain when you feel unloved or unaccepted. It means you keep your mind out of the gutter of immorality. It means you take control of your thought life.

What do you think about the most? God's hand in your everyday life? Trusting Him rather than rabbit-trailing into the what-ifs that eventually evoke fear? Or maybe, you're beginning to see the need to think on better things.

* * *

*Father, thank You for the reminder that I'm in control of my mind
and I get to choose what I think about at any given
point. In Jesus' name I pray. Amen.*

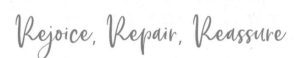

# Rejoice, Repair, Reassure

*Finally, brothers and sisters, keep rejoicing and repair whatever
is broken. Encourage each other, think as one, and live at peace;
and God, the Author of love and peace, will remain with you.*
2 CORINTHIANS 13:11 VOICE

Life can be hard and full of heartaches. On any given day, we may face broken relationships, health scares, financial trouble, loss and grief, overwhelming fears, debilitating insecurities, and a myriad of other tough battles. That's why verses like the one above can be a powerful motivator for our spirits.

We're reminded that God's presence is always with us, reassuring us when we need it most. No matter what we're going through, we can rejoice that His love and peace are always available. And it also encourages us to grab on to good community, repairing any relationship to health because they're a wonderful source of support as well.

. . . . . . . . . . . . . . . . . . . . . . . . . . . . . . . . . . . . . . . . . . . .

*Father, life may knock me down, but I have every reason
and encouragement to get up and press through it.
You've made sure of that! In Jesus' name I pray. Amen.*

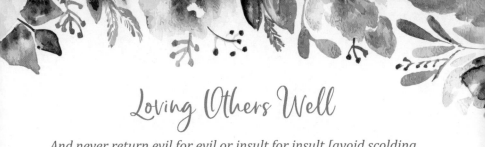

# Loving Others Well

*And never return evil for evil or insult for insult [avoid scolding, berating, and any kind of abuse], but on the contrary, give a blessing [pray for one another's well-being, contentment, and protection]; for you have been called for this very purpose, that you might inherit a blessing [from God that brings well-being, happiness, and protection].*

1 PETER 3:9 AMP

Loving others is a privilege. Show people how much they matter. Speak encouragement into the weary hearts of those who need reminders that they have what it takes. Bless someone's day by simply complimenting them or helping them. And take those you love to God's throne room in prayer, speaking their name and your request directly to the Father.

Every day, you get to choose if, how, and when to bless those around you. Your kindness and generosity can change the trajectory of someone's day.

*Father, I want to be known as a woman who loves others well. I want to bless whenever possible, helping others feel loved and seen. Help me be a blessing! In Jesus' name I pray. Amen.*

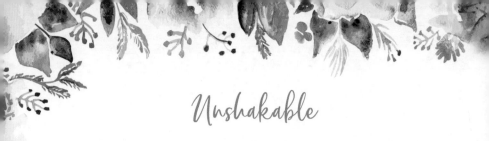

# Unshakable

*The mountains may shift, and the hills may be shaken, but my
faithful love won't shift from you, and my covenant of peace
won't be shaken, says the LORD, the one who pities you.*
ISAIAH 54:10 CEB

Everything in the world is unsteady. So when you choose to place your trust in people, processes, plans, or politics, it's guaranteed that your foundation will be shaken. Even when they have every good intention, people can be finicky and unreliable. Your fail-safe plans can falter, your impeccable organizational skills are imperfect at best, and there's no political party that has all the answers.

But God's love and peace are constant. They're unshakable—always have been, always will be. And when you need a reminder that you're loved, He will freely give it. When you need His peace, it's available 24-7. God is the only reliable One, and He is yours.

- - - - - - - - - - - - - - - - - - - - - - - - - - - - - - - - - - - - - - - -

*Father, oh how I love You. In a world that is always unsteady
and ever changing, thank You that You are not. I know
that You are all I need. In Jesus' name I pray. Amen.*

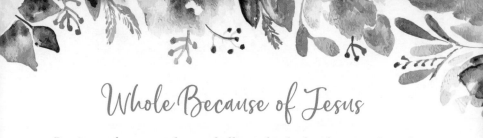

# Whole Because of Jesus

*But it was because of our rebellious deeds that he was pierced
and because of our sins that he was crushed. He endured
the punishment that made us completely whole,
and in his wounding we found our healing.*

<small>ISAIAH 53:5 TPT</small>

Jesus is the answer. He is the reason. He's why you're clean and acceptable in God's eyes. Jesus is why you're saved for eternity. He filled the gap between your sins and the Father. It's Jesus. He is the Savior of the world. He's the Savior of you.

Have you ever thanked Him? Have you sat in gratitude, considering the future He saved you from? Today, show appreciation for all He's done to make you whole. It will be time well spent, and it will remind you of the amazing Lord you serve!

*Father, You've done so much for me through Your Son.
Sometimes I forget the depth of Your love and the sacrifices
made on my behalf to ensure an eternity with You. I am full
of gratitude—now and always. In Jesus' name I pray. Amen.*

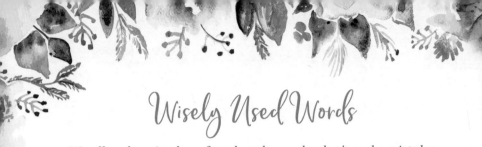

# Wisely Used Words

*We all make mistakes often, but those who don't make mistakes with their words have reached full maturity. Like a bridled horse, they can control themselves entirely.*

JAMES 3:2 CEB

Be careful with the words you speak toward others. Words have the power to pull someone from the pit of despair or push them into it. Your words can be the perfect medicine to encourage a weary heart or part of the reason depression sets in. The truth is that not every thought that comes into your mind needs to be spoken.

The wise woman knows when to speak and when to stay silent. There are times for both. She knows how to share hard things with a generous spirit. And being intentional to speak the right words at the right time shows maturity and confidence.

*Father, help me be cautious with my words. I want to make sure my tongue doesn't lash out with the wrong motives. I need wisdom and self-control. In Jesus' name I pray. Amen.*

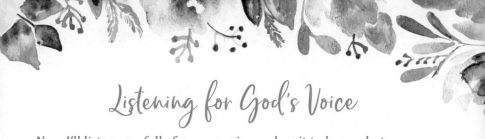

# Listening for God's Voice

*Now I'll listen carefully for your voice and wait to hear whatever you say. Let me hear your promise of peace—the message every one of your godly lovers longs to hear. Don't let us in our ignorance turn back from following you.*

PSALM 85:8 TPT

Choose to be the kind of woman who turns her ear to the Lord. It's easy for His still, small voice to get drowned out by the world—a collection of opinions, ideas, and suggestions. But the world's wisdom isn't godly, and the world's thoughts aren't always in your best interest.

Whom do you listen to the most? Do you seek your friend's advice or a family member's counsel? Do you research online, talk to a counselor, or read books for direction? While human guidance can be helpful, nothing replaces God's words. Listen carefully for His instruction and then take the next right step.

* * *

*Father, give me the ears to hear You, the patience to wait on Your words, and the wisdom to know I'm listening to the right counsel. In Jesus' name I pray. Amen.*

# God Is the Ultimate Fear Buster

*"Do not yield to fear, for I am always near. Never turn your gaze
from me, for I am your faithful God. I will infuse you with my
strength and help you in every situation. I will hold
you firmly with my victorious right hand."*
ISAIAH 41:10 TPT

Fear is a big deal. Chances are it informs many of your decisions. It's easy to look down the road and predict horrible outcomes to any situation. We can think back to all the times we tried and failed, and it leaves us scared to try again. Yes, fear really is a big deal.

But if you take those things that scare you to God, He promises to infuse you with His strength. He pledges His help in every intimidating situation you have to face. And what's more, God guarantees His presence and victory every time.

* * * * * * * * * * * * * * * * * * * * * * * * * * * * * * * * * * * *

*Father, I confess that I've lived in fear for as long as I can remember.
I need the kind of courage and confidence only You offer.
Please help me. In Jesus' name I pray. Amen.*

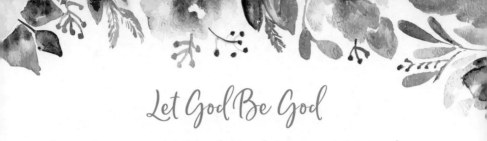

# Let God Be God

*Surrender your anxiety! Be silent and stop your striving and you will see that I am God. I am the God above all the nations, and I will be exalted throughout the whole earth.*

PSALM 46:10 TPT

God is God and you are not. Maybe that bears repeating. . .out loud this time? As women, we are a force to be reckoned with. We can multitask with the best of them and are adept at running the world around us. Between family, career, school, and all that's required to run a home, we might begin to feel godlike. But we're not.

God is asking you to surrender to His will and ways, to be silent long enough to hear His direction, and to stop trying so hard to have everything under your control. Let God be God, and rest knowing you are not.

• • • • • • • • • • • • • • • • • • • • • • • • • • • • • • • • • • • • • • • • •

*Father, forgive me for not including You in my plans. I'm sorry for those times I've forgotten that You are God—not me. Help me live in daily worship of You! In Jesus' name I pray. Amen.*

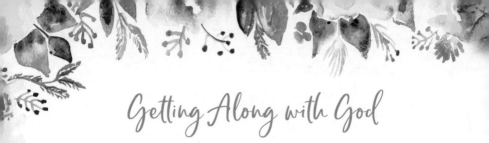

# Getting Along with God

*Get along well with God and be at peace;*
*from this something good will come to you.*

JOB 22:21 CEB

At some point we have to choose to trust God's plan and purpose for our lives. We may have had something different in mind as we reached adulthood, but choosing to surrender our half-baked ideas to the Father's perfect plan keeps us at peace with Him.

The truth is that His plans are better than our plans and His ways are far better than our ways. What if instead of getting frustrated with Him we decided to trust? What would happen if we decided to wait for Him to reveal our next steps rather than just doing what we wanted?

It would create harmony and peace with our Daddy. And that would be epic.

* * * * * * * * * * * * * * * * * * * * * * * * * * * * * * * * * * * * * * * *

*Father, I believe that You have good things planned for me.*
*Forgive me for bypassing Your blueprint and mapping out*
*my own way. More than anything else, I want to be at*
*peace with You! In Jesus' name I pray. Amen.*

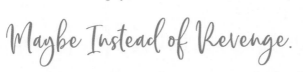

# Maybe Instead of Revenge. . .

*Resist revenge, and make sure that no one pays back evil in place
of evil but always pursue doing what is beautiful to
one another and to all the unbelievers.*

1 Thessalonians 5:15 tpt

Sometimes the idea of revenge is sweet. Have you ever sat and plotted the perfect words you'd say to the person who hurt you, or concocted the perfect plan to give someone a taste of their own medicine? Somehow, the idea of this makes us feel better—at least for a while.

Those thoughts aren't something God wants you to spend time on. Maybe instead of revenge, God wants you to know He sees every injustice and promises to handle them on your behalf. He wants you to pursue kindness and compassion toward others. And He wants you to bring beauty into the world with your love.

*Father, I want to be a woman known for her kindness and
generosity. I want my words and actions to point others
to You, Lord. In Jesus' name I pray. Amen.*

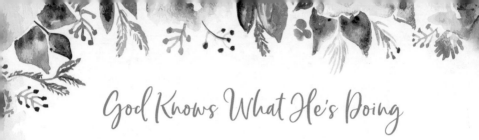

# God Knows What He's Doing

*"I know what I'm doing. I have it all planned out—plans to take care of you, not abandon you, plans to give you the future you hope for."*
JEREMIAH 29:11 MSG

*The Message* translation of this verse brings it to life in a new way. It's a refreshing reminder of something so obvious and yet so easily overlooked: God knows what He is doing.

That means you don't have to worry about the future. You don't have to be anxious about how you'll make ends meet or if you'll get the job. There's no need to take control of the situation or try to manipulate your way to a solution. He's planned it all out, and everything is going to work out. Deep breath. . .God's got this.

. . . . . . . . . . . . . . . . . . . . . . . . . . . . . . . . . . . . . . . . .

*Father, thank You for knowing what You're doing! Help me find rest in that truth so I don't feel the pressure to be a playmaker or fear what's ahead. I want to trust You in everything. In Jesus' name I pray. Amen.*

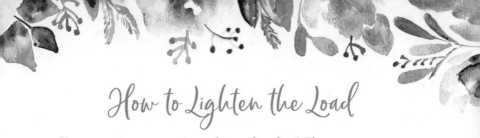

# How to Lighten the Load

*"Are you weary, carrying a heavy burden? Then come to me.*
*I will refresh your life, for I am your oasis."*
MATTHEW 11:28 TPT

What weighs heavy on your heart today? Is it feeling left out of a friendship? Is your marriage on the rocks, or are you having a hard time getting pregnant? Maybe your finances are a mess or the doctor called with disheartening news. Or it could be anger from unforgiveness, hurt from reckless words, or a million other things.

God wants you to give those burdens to Him so He can lighten your load. He's ready to hear your heart and bring you peace and comfort this very moment. And when you tell Him all that's going on, a supernatural sense of relief washes over you. The problem may not be gone, but your weary spirit is refreshed. Give it a try.

. . . . . . . . . . . . . . . . . . . . . . . . . . . . . . . . . . . . . .

*Father, I'm buckling under the weight of disappointment and hurt.*
*I need renewed strength for the battle. Thank You for hearing my*
*heart and promising to bring relief. In Jesus' name I pray. Amen.*

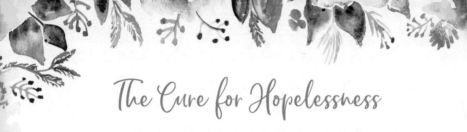

# The Cure for Hopelessness

*Don't get lost in despair; believe in God,*
*and keep on believing in Me.*
JOHN 14:1 VOICE

Feeling hopeless is a deep pit that's hard to climb out of. It's like a dense cloud covering that dampens everything. It leaves you feeling miserable, robbing you of the joy and peace that usually mark your day. And if you let it, it will ruin your life.

But God knew despair was something we'd all face in this imperfect world full of imperfect people. So rather than leave us to figure it out ourselves, He purposefully inked the remedy right onto the pages of His Word. Jesus said we need to believe that He see us, that He knows what we need, and that He'll provide hope if we trust Him rather than getting lost in hopelessness. We must activate our faith over the pull to give up.

* * * * * * * * * * * * * * * * * * * * * * * * * * * * * * * * * * * *

*Father, sometimes I don't see the light at the end of the tunnel*
*and it discourages me. Help me trust You in those circumstances*
*where I'm losing hope. In Jesus' name I pray. Amen.*

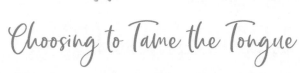

# Choosing to Tame the Tongue

*For let him who wants to enjoy life and see good days [good—
whether apparent or not] keep his tongue free from evil
and his lips from guile (treachery, deceit).*

1 Peter 3:10 AMPC

The tongue has a way of getting us in trouble, doesn't it? Too often we're quick to lash out at someone who has hurt us, or we want to have the last word during an argument. We don't think before we speak and end up using words as weapons. Or we make someone feel small and worthless as we seek revenge.

But God wants our words to glorify Him, whether we're encouraging a friend through a tough season or having a hard conversation with a coworker. No matter the situation, we can access self-control and kindness so our words affirm rather than annihilate.

*Father, I confess there are times I want my words to sting. Sometimes I say things just to hurt the other person. Please forgive me. I want to live in peace. Help me tame my tongue. In Jesus' name I pray. Amen.*

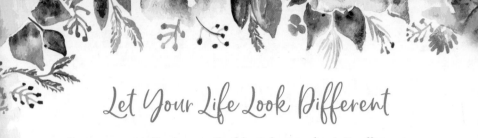

# Let Your Life Look Different

*But you can tell who are the blameless and spiritually mature.*
*What a different story with them! The godly ones will have*
*a peaceful, prosperous future with a happy ending.*

Psalm 37:37 TPT

The goal of your life is to have your words and actions point others to God. The faithful are His Plan A. We are the ones who will share Jesus with the world. There is no Plan B. How you live your life matters because it preaches, whether you realize it or not.

Would others know you love the Lord by the choices you make? Does your calendar and checkbook reflect the value you place on your faith? This isn't a call to be perfect, but it is a reminder to live with purpose. Remember that people are watching how you live and love, and your authentic heart will glorify the Lord in heaven.

*Father, I want others to see You because of my words and actions.*
*Help me be the right kind of witness at the right*
*time. In Jesus' name I pray. Amen.*

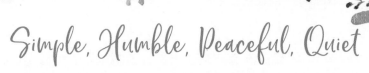

# Simple, Humble, Peaceful, Quiet

*A simple, humble life with peace and quiet is far better than an opulent lifestyle with nothing but quarrels and strife at home.*

PROVERBS 17:1 TPT

This proverb isn't suggesting you hole up in your home and live alone. It isn't saying you shouldn't have good friends and family around. And it doesn't mean you'll only be happy if your home is silent and your belongings sparse. No, ma'am.

But there is a state of chaos that naturally surrounds living in the fast lane. It can become a rat race just to keep up with the Joneses, and we often develop—sometimes without even realizing it—a desire for more, bigger, and better. It stirs up dissention and unrest in our souls.

Ask God for contentment so you can live in peace. He is all you really need.

· · · · · · · · · · · · · · · · · · · · · · · · · · · · · · · · · · · · ·

*Father, more than anything else, I want to stay in Your peace. I want to live in a place of contentment. And I don't want to strive for more, unless it's more of You. In Jesus' name I pray. Amen.*

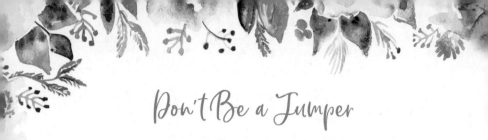

# Don't Be a Jumper

*Honor is due those who refuse to fight at the drop of a hat,
but every fool jumps at an opportunity to quarrel.*

PROVERBS 20:3 VOICE

Sometimes it feels good to fight—to just let someone have it—especially when we're already feeling cranky. There are moments when it doesn't take much to set us off, and engaging in an argument feels justified. It feels warranted. And rather than have a productive conversation laced with truth and love, we pounce on someone.

But God delights in us when we're slow to anger. It may be the right emotion for the situation we are facing, but that doesn't mean it should always be acted on. When we're quick to jump into rage, it pulls us from the peace of Jesus.

* * *

*Father, I confess that I like a good fight sometimes. And I don't always fight fair. But I don't want to be a jumper. Instead, I want to be slow to anger because I don't want to live outside of Your peace. In Jesus' name I pray. Amen.*

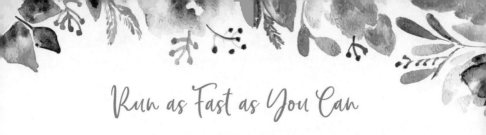

# Run as Fast as You Can

*Run as fast as you can from all the ambitions and lusts of youth;
and chase after all that is pure. Whatever builds up your faith and
deepens your love must become your holy pursuit. And live in peace
with all those who worship our Lord Jesus with pure hearts.*

2 Timothy 2:22 TPT

Simply put, we're to run (not lollygag) as fast as our legs will take us
from immaturity. There's just no place for it in our lives. God is asking
us to pursue good things—things that increase our faith, grow our love
for Him and others, and keep us in the peace of Jesus.

You'll find maturity in prayer and time spent in God's Word. You'll
find it as you get to know God more intimately. Developing friendships
with like-minded women will help, as will finding ways to serve those
in need. Run after these things.

*Father, sometimes I need a reminder not to chase after the wrong
things. Help me live a holy pursuit. In Jesus' name I pray. Amen.*

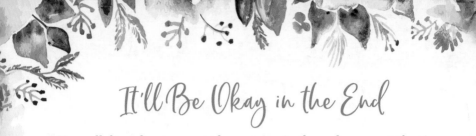

# It'll Be Okay in the End

*Now all discipline seems to be more pain than pleasure at the time, yet later it will produce a transformation of character, bringing a harvest of righteousness and peace to those who yield to it.*

HEBREWS 12:11 TPT

No one actually enjoys being corrected. For many, even constructive criticism is a hard pill to swallow. But if the goal is to perfect our faith and make us more like Jesus, we'll have to be open to making adjustments in how we're living.

Divine discipline happens because character matters. It's what others see in you that has the God-powered ability to make them want to know Him. And He loves you too much to leave you where you are. When you say yes to Him, God will work in your heart and life to bring forth the fruit He planned for you. Trust Him.

*Father, I don't enjoy the correction process. Life is hard enough without feeling like a failure. Please give me humility to know You discipline in love. In Jesus' name I pray. Amen.*

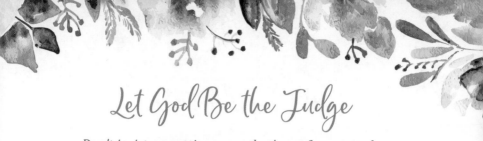

# Let God Be the Judge

*Don't insist on getting even; that's not for you to do.*
*"I'll do the judging," says God. "I'll take care of it."*
ROMANS 12:19 MSG

If we were to be honest, we'd all admit there are times we just want to get even. When someone hurts us or someone we love, our mama-bear claws come out and people would be smart to head for the hills. Amen? But God tells us that He will take care of the injustice. He reminds us that He will be the One to judge, so we can step off the bench and out of the courtroom altogether.

Trust the Lord and give Him space to work things out on your behalf. He absolutely will. Haven't you seen it before? Can't you recall a time when God intervened? He will continue to stand for you, friend. And when He does, it allows you to stay in peace because He has your back.

*Father, thank You for being a God of justice. I trust You to*
*take care of things. In Jesus' name I pray. Amen.*

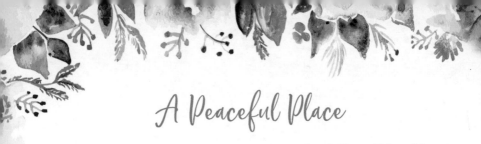

# A Peaceful Place

*I will see to it that you have peace in your land. You will be able to go to bed at night without a worry on your mind. I will take away the dangerous animals that roam your land, and no armies will invade your land.*

LEVITICUS 26:6 VOICE

Doesn't this verse paint the picture of a beautiful place? It's almost garden of Eden-ish. With the chaos of our world, the endless fighting and bickering, and those things that create worry and anxiety in our hearts, we're desperate for a peaceful place.

Here's what's awesome. Even with all the crazy, you can live in harmony anyway. With the peace of Jesus, it's possible for you to stay calm when everything around you feels chaotic and overwhelming. It's possible to have a quiet heart when you're standing in the middle of a life storm. And friend, He is the way.

. . . . . . . . . . . . . . . . . . . . . . . . . . . . . . . . . . . . . . . . . .

*Father, I need You to bring peace into my heart. It's weary, and I'm tired. Please bring me to a peaceful place with You. In Jesus' name I pray. Amen.*

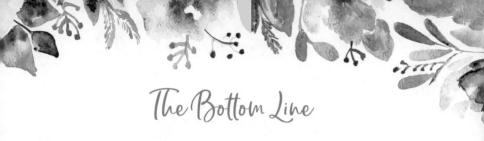

# The Bottom Line

*Here is the bottom line: do not worry about your life. Don't worry about what you will eat or what you will drink. Don't worry about how you clothe your body. Living is about more than merely eating, and the body is about more than dressing up.*

MATTHEW 6:25 VOICE

The Lord's words are simple to hear but hard to walk out. How are we supposed to *not worry* when we're moms raising kids, or daughters with aging parents? How can we stay calm when our marriage is falling apart, or we can't seem to find someone to marry? How do we live without anxiety when the diagnosis comes, or finances fail?

Jesus. He's the One who came so we could live in freedom, and that includes freedom from worry. When you feel troubled, ask God to comfort you. Ask for the peace of Jesus to rest on you. And tell God you trust Him to handle it all.

· · · · · · · · · · · · · · · · · · · · · · · · · · · · · · · · · · ·

*Father, my heart is uneasy. Too many things are causing anxiety. Please help me. In Jesus' name I pray. Amen.*

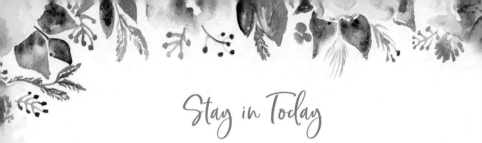

# Stay in Today

*"Refuse to worry about tomorrow, but deal with each challenge that comes your way, one day at a time. Tomorrow will take care of itself."*
MATTHEW 6:34 TPT

One of the Enemy's greatest schemes is enticing us to look far down the road and imagine nothing but horrible outcomes. We look at where we are today and the end results we want, and it feels hopeless. It looks impossible. And rather than concentrate on taking the next right step, we freeze up.

Jesus offers the perfect solution, and it's choosing to stay in today. He knows our tendency as women to carry the weight of the world on our shoulders and drown in worry. But if we take His advice and choose to deal only with today's troubles, it's manageable. It's bite-size. And it will keep us from being overwhelmed with tomorrow's problems.

* * * * * * * * * * * * * * * * * * * * * * * * * * * * * * * * * * * * * * * *

*Father, I tend to bite off more than I can chew and it stirs up worry and anxiety. Help me follow Your ways and stay present in today. In Jesus' name I pray. Amen.*

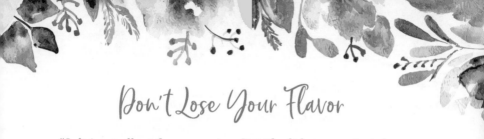

# Don't Lose Your Flavor

*"Salt is excellent for seasoning. But if salt becomes tasteless, how can its flavor ever be restored? Your lives, like salt, are to season and preserve. So don't lose your flavor, and preserve the peace in your union with one another."*

MARK 9:50 TPT

You bring a unique flavor to the world. There never was, is, or will be anyone exactly like you to walk planet Earth. When God thought you up, He was on His A game. Oh yes, there is so much goodness inside of you, friend.

Be careful not to lose your flavor. Don't get so bogged down with the stressors and struggles of life that you become bland. Don't allow bitterness to rule. Refuse any sprinkling of unforgiveness in your heart. Live at peace whenever possible. And never change the essence of who God made you to be, because it's awesome.

* * *

*Father, thank You for making me a unique blend of seasoning! Would You give me confidence to bring my sweet and spicy mix into everything I do? In Jesus' name I pray. Amen.*

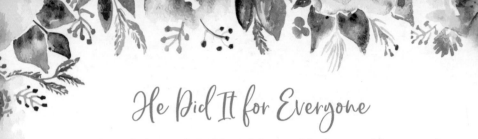

# He Did It for Everyone

*"For this is how much God loved the world—he gave his one and only, unique Son as a gift. So now everyone who believes in him will never perish but experience everlasting life."*

JOHN 3:16 TPT

When Jesus was nailed to the cross, it was for everyone—past, present, future. He died for abusive parents. He died for ex-husbands. Jesus died for mean-spirited coworkers and hateful landlords. He gave His life for the driver who cut us off and the dismissive doctor at the clinic. Jesus hung on that cross so we *all* could have eternal life.

Even when you're spittin' mad at someone's response or offended by how you've been treated, Jesus loves that person just as much as He loves you. Having that perspective helps, because if God has forgiven them. . .you can as well. And it offers a gentle reminder that you're in need of a Savior too.

. . . . . . . . . . . . . . . . . . . . . . . . . . . . . . . . . . . . . .

*Father, thank You for Jesus. And thank You for loving me enough to send Him to a cross. In Jesus' name I pray. Amen.*

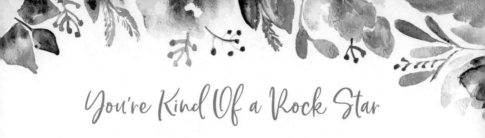

# You're Kind Of a Rock Star

*You see, God did not give us a cowardly spirit*
*but a powerful, loving, and disciplined spirit.*
2 TIMOTHY 1:7 VOICE

You're not a coward—no way, nohow. Think of all the brave things you did just last week. Maybe you got out of bed when you wanted to sleep in. Maybe you advocated for yourself when it would have been easier to keep your mouth shut, or you took on something new that felt scary. Maybe you had a hard conversation and kept your cool. And that's just the tip of the iceberg.

You see, God never intended for you to be spineless and weak. He made you powerful so you'd have the grit to trust even when scared. He loved you first so you could pass it on. And God gave you motivation and confidence to keep trying. Yeah, you're kind of a rock star.

· · · · · · · · · · · · · · · · · · · · · · · · · · · · · · · · · · · · · · · ·

*Father, I am not a coward. And I'm thankful that You made*
*me with the guts and grit to not back down or give*
*in. In Jesus' name I pray. Amen.*

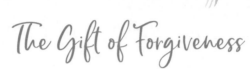

# The Gift of Forgiveness

*Tolerate the weaknesses of those in the family of faith,
forgiving one another in the same way you have been graciously
forgiven by Jesus Christ. If you find fault with someone,
release this same gift of forgiveness to them.*

COLOSSIANS 3:13 TPT

When you hold on to unforgiveness, you're putting yourself in a prison. And you're being held by bitterness and anger, something that only hurts you. Refusing to extend grace is bad for you because it eats away at peace. It keeps you stirred up and joyless. You may think it's hurting the other person, but the real victim is you.

Forgiving others doesn't mean what they did was right, nor does it make the pain you feel invalid. But when you choose to release the offense from your heart, you're making a conscious decision to stay in God's peace. And there's no place you'd rather be.

* * *

*Father, I confess that I struggle to forgive others. It's so easy to
live offended, and I need Your help to release the pain
and hurt. In Jesus' name I pray. Amen.*

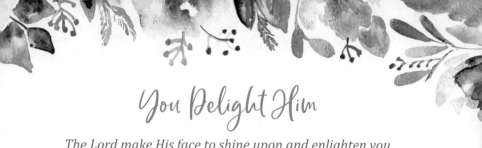

# You Delight Him

*The Lord make His face to shine upon and enlighten you
and be gracious (kind, merciful, and giving favor) to you.*

NUMBERS 6:25 AMPC

God's favor is on you because you are His child. You are His masterpiece. He never looks away from you in disgust when you mess up because He sees you through the blood of His Son, Jesus. You are perfect in His eyes. His love shines down on you because He delights in who you are—stumbles, fumbles, and all. You are adored.

So when the world is mean-spirited and you feel judged, when people let you down and you feel discarded, when nothing seems to go right and you want to give up, remember that your Father in heaven sees you. He is forever kindhearted and compassionate when it comes to you, and He's always available. And even when it seems like no one else sees your value and worth, you never fail to delight Him.

. . . . . . . . . . . . . . . . . . . . . . . . . . . . . . . . . . . . . . . .

*Father, I love You. I'm humbled by how much
You love me. In Jesus' name I pray. Amen.*

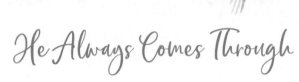

# He Always Comes Through

*Eventually, they will all give you trouble, but you will be safe.*
*They will fight you, but they will not win. Remember,*
*I am with you. I promise I will always deliver you.*
JEREMIAH 1:19 VOICE

This epic promise has a powerful calming effect on our hearts. It's a reminder that out of the crazy and messy, God will come through for us. Again. He's letting us know that at the end of the day, His will. . .will come to pass. The Lord's words here are designed to straighten our backs for battle. He's offering divine perspective.

Life may feel real big right now and your joy may be drained. There may be a heavy burden of reality sitting on your chest that's making it hard to catch a breath. People you once trusted may be letting you down left and right. And others may be waging a war against you—one you never saw coming and feel ill prepared to fight. But friend, God's got you.

. . . . . . . . . . . . . . . . . . . . . . . . . . . . . . . . . . . . . . . . .

*Father, I'm so grateful Your promises never fail.*
*In Jesus' name I pray. Amen.*

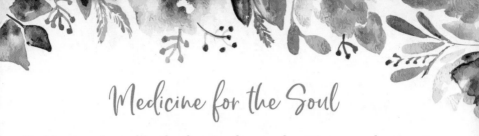

# Medicine for the Soul

*Reckless words are like the thrusts of a sword, cutting remarks meant to stab and to hurt. But the words of the wise soothe and heal.*

PROVERBS 12:18 TPT

Your words matter more than you may think. Whether spoken out loud, written on a page, or thought in your mind, they matter. Sometimes we make cutting remarks thoughtlessly or as a "joke," and it cuts deep. And other times we know exactly what we're doing as we weaponize our words to hurt others.

Be the kind of woman who uses her words wisely. Just as they can cut others, words also have the power to bring life and hope to those who need it the most. They can turn someone's day around for the better. Kind words are medicine for the soul. Use them with care.

. . . . . . . . . . . . . . . . . . . . . . . . . . . . . . . . . . . . . .

*Father, from this day forward, I'm choosing to let my words be medicinal. I confess I've been reckless in the past, but I'm changing that. In Jesus' name I pray. Amen.*

# Your Heart Shapes Your Words

*Be gracious in your speech. The goal is to bring out the best in others in a conversation, not put them down, not cut them out.*
COLOSSIANS 4:6 MSG

What thoughts are swirling in you these days? Are you chewing on that situation over and over again, the one that made you spittin' mad? Are you obsessing over how someone offended you, thinking of clever ways to get even? Are you feeling sorry for yourself and talking about it to anyone who will listen?

Whatever fills your heart shapes your words. If you decide to fill your heart with the good things—the God things—it will flow out in your speech. If you breathe in His goodness and marinate in His faithfulness, that's what you'll exhale. If you focus on mercy, kindness, and generosity, you won't get tripped up by gossip, judgment, and pride.

. . . . . . . . . . . . . . . . . . . . . . . . . . . . . . . . . . . . . . . .

*Father, help me keep my heart free from offense so generous and gracious words flow from my mouth. Help me focus on the God things. In Jesus' name I pray. Amen.*

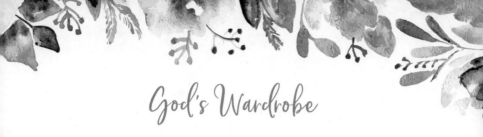

# God's Wardrobe

*So, chosen by God for this new life of love, dress in the wardrobe*
*God picked out for you: compassion, kindness, humility,*
*quiet strength, discipline.*

COLOSSIANS 3:12 MSG

Sometimes we don't want to wear what God has picked out for us. Sometimes we deliberately wear anger, hate, pride, annoyance, and impatience. We pick up offenses and stew. We gossip and obsess. We justify and get all stirred up.

But, if we don't live differently than the rest of the world, how will our words and actions point others to God? Because, friend, that's the goal for our lives. We're His Plan A for sharing Jesus with others.

Ask God to fill you with compassion, kindness, humility, quiet strength, and discipline. How you choose to live preaches one way or another.

. . . . . . . . . . . . . . . . . . . . . . . . . . . . . . . . . . . . . . . . . . .

*Father, I want to wear these things so I can love others well. I want to*
*live out my faith, focused on what's important to You. And I'm going*
*to need Your help to make it happen. In Jesus' name I pray. Amen.*

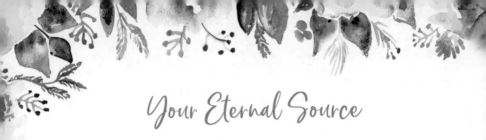

# Your Eternal Source

*Human beings are frail and temporary, like grass, and the glory of man fleeting like blossoms of the field. The grass dries and withers and the flowers fall off, but the Word of the Lord endures forever! And this is the Word that was announced to you!*

1 PETER 1:24–25 TPT

Who's your source for hope? Think about it. Finances may fail, relationships may end, and health may decline. But God is constant. He has been, He is, and He always will be. He never changes. So if you anchor your faith to anyone or anything of the world, you'll eventually find yourself adrift—hopeless, fearful, and insecure—because they're temporary. But God is your eternal source.

You can't put your faith in money, doctors, husbands, kids, political parties, movements, workouts, careers, or friends. They may be awesome and helpful, but they are not your source. Everything earthly will fade, but God endures. Let your soul rest in Him alone.

. . . . . . . . . . . . . . . . . . . . . . . . . . . . . . . . . . . . . . . . . .

*Father, You're my eternal source, and my hope rests in You! In Jesus' name I pray. Amen.*

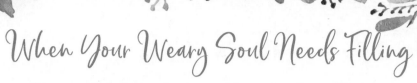

# When Your Weary Soul Needs Filling

*Now may God, the inspiration and fountain of hope, fill you to overflowing with uncontainable joy and perfect peace as you trust in him. And may the power of the Holy Spirit continually surround your life with his super-abundance until you radiate with hope!*

ROMANS 15:13 TPT

Do you need a big dose of hope, joy, and peace today? Are you perplexed by the people in your life? Discouraged by their decisions? Overwhelmed by their opinions? Hurt by their habits? Scared of the solution? Infuriated by the injustice? Guilt-ridden for giving in? Shamed by the situation? Suffering because of their stupidity? Cranky from the compromise?

Every day, there are countless ways joy is drained, hope dries up, and peace eludes us. Life is full of disappointing situations and people. And sometimes it takes all we have to hold on. Today, let the God of hope fill your weary soul with His goodness.

*Father, I feel empty and overwhelmed. Would You please fill me with Your hope, joy, and peace! In Jesus' name I pray. Amen.*

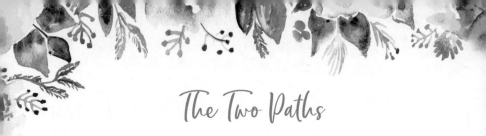

# The Two Paths

*There are two paths before you; you may take only one path.*
*One doorway is narrow. And one door is wide. Go through the narrow*
*door. For the wide door leads to a wide path, and the wide path*
*is broad; the wide, broad path is easy, and the wide, broad,*
*easy path has many, many people on it; but the wide,*
*broad, easy, crowded path leads to death.*
MATTHEW 7:13 VOICE

Friend, choose God's way. It will be a harder choice, it may be an unpopular decision, and it might be terribly inconvenient, but the narrow path of faithfulness is full of His goodness.

The narrow path will keep you right with the Lord and in His peace. But it won't only yield blessings for you and those you love; choosing it will be a bold voice of truth to the world. And the world needs to know there's a better way. Show them.

*Father, please give me courage and confidence to follow Your ways*
*no matter what others think. In Jesus' name I pray. Amen.*

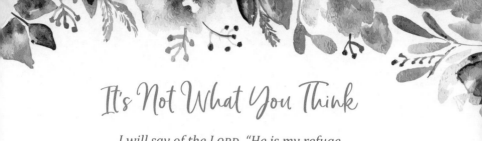

# It's Not What You Think

*I will say of the LORD, "He is my refuge*
*and my fortress, my God, in whom I trust."*
**PSALM 91:2 NIV**

It's God alone. Not any friend or mentor. Not your health. Not a trust fund. Not your career. Not your best-laid plans. Not your husband, children, or parents. Not your reputation. Not your pride. Not human-fueled grit. Not clean livin'. Not a gated community. No level of education. No political party. No church denomination. No twelve-step group or self-help book. While some of these may be good options to living and loving well. . .they're not your savior.

There is only one God, and He is always attentive. He always cares about your needs and knows what gaps to fill. He sees where you fall short, how much more you can take, and at what point you will break. The Lord is the only safe place—your only capable Protector—and He always will be.

. . . . . . . . . . . . . . . . . . . . . . . . . . . . . . . . . . . . . . . . .

*Father, You are my refuge and fortress. Help me trust in*
*You and not the world. In Jesus' name I pray. Amen.*

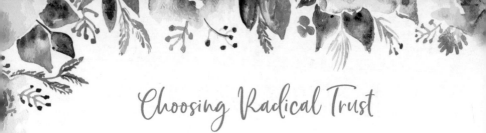

# Choosing Radical Trust

*The Lord is my Shepherd [to feed, guide,
and shield me], I shall not lack.*
PSALM 23:1 AMPC

Here's what the psalmist knew that we often forget. God is our source. Through Him, we can live contented lives because He promises to give us what we need. We don't have to waste time worrying. We don't have to obsess about essentials and necessities. Instead, we can choose to trust that what we have today is all we need and that God will meet our needs tomorrow.

This radical trust isn't always easy, but it's absolutely necessary for a peaceful and content heart. Don't worry, friend. God sees you. He knows what you need. And even more, He wants you to trust Him enough to care for you. He promises to. So choose to believe He's your source, and watch Him prove you right.

. . . . . . . . . . . . . . . . . . . . . . . . . . . . . . . . . . . . . . . . . . .

*Father, I confess there are times I doubt Your ability and willingness
to provide for me. Would You increase my faith so I have radical
trust in Your love for me? In Jesus' name I pray. Amen.*

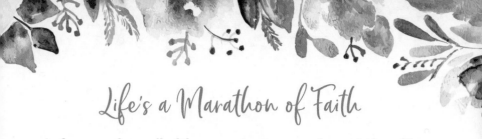

# Life's a Marathon of Faith

*As for us, we have all of these great witnesses who encircle us like clouds. So we must let go of every wound that has pierced us and the sin we so easily fall into. Then we will be able to run life's marathon race with passion and determination, for the path has been already marked out before us.*

HEBREWS 12:1 TPT

You may want to quit a marriage or walk away from a dream. You may want to give in to the addiction or blow your budget. You may even want to stop trying for that hard-to-reach goal. But friend, if God called you to it. . .somehow, someway, He will equip you to endure through it. With His help, you can keep going. Don't let anyone tell you different—not even your own self.

So lace up your shoes. Fill up your water bottle. Grab a snack. And stay the course.

*Father, I need Your strength and wisdom to keep going.
I cannot do it without You. In Jesus' name I pray. Amen.*

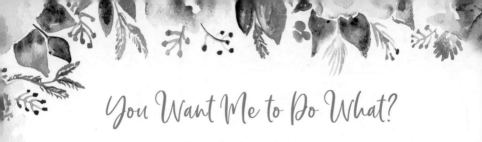

# You Want Me to Do What?

*"However, I say to you, love your enemy, bless the one who curses you,*
*do something wonderful for the one who hates you, and respond*
*to the very ones who persecute you by praying for them."*

MATTHEW 5:44 TPT

This verse is the antidote to hate. It's what keeps you from living offended. It's how you stay positive, compassionate, gracious, and effective for the kingdom. It's simple. . .and not so simple at the same time.

Here's how you put God's command into practice. Do you despise her? Then pray for the grace to love. Are you furious at them? Then pray for a heart of reconciliation. Do you feel belittled by him? Then pray for God to change his focus.

This isn't about being a doormat for abuse. Healthy boundaries are vital to emotional health. But when you love and pray for your enemies, it takes the power away from them and keeps you from becoming bitter and angry.

. . . . . . . . . . . . . . . . . . . . . . . . . . . . . . . . . . . . . . . . . .

*Father, please help me. I can't do this without You.*
*In Jesus' name I pray. Amen.*

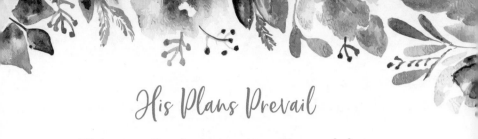

# His Plans Prevail

*We humans keep brainstorming options and plans,*
*but GOD's purpose prevails.*
PROVERBS 19:21 MSG

The simple (yet hard to understand) truth is that God's plans are often very different from the plans we've cooked up for ourselves. We have limited vision for our lives and future. And while we can't see what's down the road, God can. He can see it because He planned it. And it's spectacular.

Don't stop dreaming though. God gave you a creative mind and wants you to use it. And don't stop trying new things as you seek out your purpose. God loves forward motion, and He delights in your passion and eagerness.

But He does want you to yield to the plans He created for your life—ones full of hope. God isn't an innocent bystander, waiting to see how everything will turn out. God isn't crossing His fingers in expectation. God has a beautiful purpose for you, and it will prevail.

*Father, I will follow where You lead. I'm excited for*
*what's ahead! In Jesus' name I pray. Amen.*

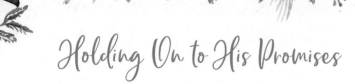

# Holding On to His Promises

*"Behold—God is my salvation! I am confident, unafraid,*
*and I will trust in you." Yes! The Lord Yah is my might*
*and my melody; he has become my salvation!*
ISAIAH 12:2 TPT

If we were to be truthful, we'd agree this verse is difficult to walk out on the regular. We may muster grit to trust that God will give us what we need for the battle, but we do so full of fear and anxiety. Or we might find guts to navigate a joy-draining situation, but we're riddled with insecurity instead of confidence.

But this verse is a promise. It's an anchor to secure us when the storms of life threaten to pull us under. And when we believe these words and hold on for dear life, we look back and see all the ways God kept the promise. We see how we were rescued. We're affirmed by the courage and conviction we saw in ourselves. And we have gratitude for the ways God was trustworthy.

*Father, I believe in and trust You. . .no matter what.*
*In Jesus' name I pray. Amen.*

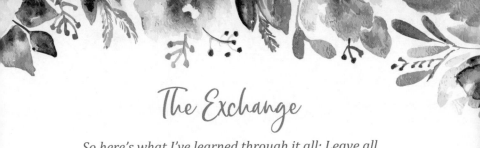

# The Exchange

*So here's what I've learned through it all: Leave all your cares and anxieties at the feet of the Lord, and measureless grace will strengthen you.*

Psalm 55:22 tpt

These words can feel very Christianese. It's advice people may offer when you're struggling, and it can often feel like a quick response so they don't have to listen to your heartache. But it's not a Christian platitude. It's a big truth.

This is deep, raw truth and hard-won wisdom. It takes guts to do, and grit to continue doing, when life feels overwhelming. It's scary to release control and put your fearful heart into the hands of someone you cannot see or touch. But when you do, the results are epic.

Your heart is safe with God. And you can confidently make this exchange because His shoulders are broader, His strength is greater, and His solutions are better.

. . . . . . . . . . . . . . . . . . . . . . . . . . . . . . . . . . . . . . . .

*Father, I willingly give You my anxieties. Please fill me with grace and strength to keep going. In Jesus' name I pray. Amen.*

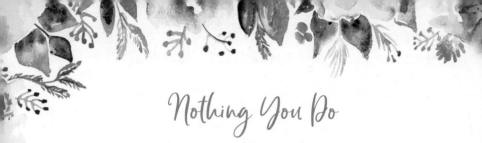

# Nothing You Do

*The Lord appeared to them from a distance: I have loved you
with a love that lasts forever. And so with unfailing
love, I have drawn you to myself.*

Jeremiah 31:3 ceb

God's love never runs out. He never gets to the end of His rope with
you. His love isn't dependent on what you do. . .or don't do. There are
no heavenly eye rolls in frustration. His back is never turned to you.
His gaze is locked on you. God never considers walking away. You're
not too much or too little. He doesn't wish you were someone else.
God is not put out with you.

Even when you mess up, collect offenses, hate others, walk away,
abandon responsibilities, spread gossip, embrace lies, or hold on to
anger. . .His love for you is and will always be unfailing. And sweet one,
there's nothing you can do to change His mind.

· · · · · · · · · · · · · · · · · · · · · · · · · · · · · · · · · · · · · ·

*Father, thank You for loving me so fiercely. Help me remember that
Your love isn't dependent on my actions. In Jesus' name I pray. Amen.*

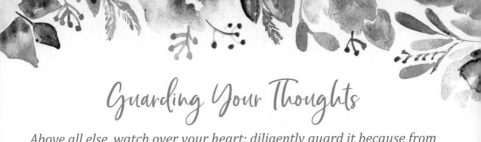

# Guarding Your Thoughts

*Above all else, watch over your heart; diligently guard it because from*
*a sincere and pure heart come the good and noble things of life.*
PROVERBS 4:23 VOICE

When you guard your heart, you're guarding your thoughts. It's your mind God is telling you to protect. And there's nothing passive about this command. It requires something from you.

It means stopping the negative self-talk, internal rants, judgmental mind-set, self-loathing, and destructive banter in your brain. Because, make no mistake, your thoughts inform your actions. You will act out how you think and feel.

So friend, be sure to guard those thoughts. The ones you choose to embrace will absolutely determine how you live your one and only life. And know that being protective will help you embrace the beautiful life God intended, even with all the ups and downs that come with it.

*Father, I will guard my heart and mind. I'm glad to know the*
*connection, and it makes sense. Help me be aware of my thoughts*
*so I live and love well. In Jesus' name I pray. Amen.*

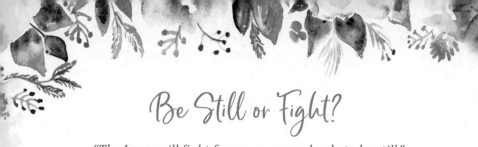

# Be Still or Fight?

*"The LORD will fight for you; you need only to be still."*
EXODUS 14:14 NIV

Moses spoke these words to the fearful Israelites as they stood with an army behind them and the Red Sea before them. They were desperate for a miracle. And God delivered. The sea split open and they walked to freedom on dry ground.

Sometimes we're required to fight the battle ourselves, speak up and advocate, courageously stand our ground, and persevere as long as it takes. And other times we are to be patient and trusting, keeping our mouths shut and staying calm, and surrendering control as our Father battles on our behalf.

Both are difficult and necessitate epic faith. Both require obedience. Both are choices we have to make. And we need God to help us walk each of them out.

Next time you are facing a battle, ask yourself: Is God asking me to fight this or be still and let Him?

*Father, give me the ears and eyes to know Your will for me in the battles I face. In Jesus' name I pray. Amen.*

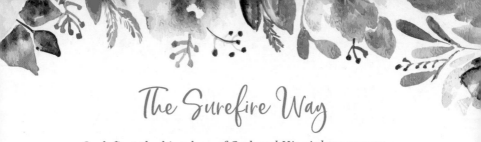

# The Surefire Way

*Seek first the kingdom of God and His righteousness,
and then all these things will be given to you too.*
MATTHEW 6:33 VOICE

Talk about a surefire way to living a faithful life—a life that benefits you and glorifies God. The truth is, it's not always an easy choice. This kind of focus requires you to put aside your fleshly desires, lofty ideals, self-importance, and big plans. Instead you surrender to God, seeking His will, His plan, His desire and direction, His wisdom, and His hope for your life.

The deeper we fall into this beautiful relationship with God, the more we understand one important thing: It's not about us. It's about Him. And when we live that way, we find that our focus isn't on what we do or do not have. We don't feel entitled or pout about missing out on things. And there's no hint of a victim mentality. We are seeking His ways above ours, and our hearts are full.

. . . . . . . . . . . . . . . . . . . . . . . . . . . . . . . . . . . . .

*Father, every day, help me seek You above everything else.
In Jesus' name I pray. Amen.*

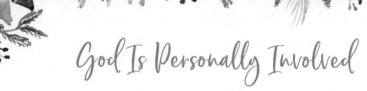

# God Is Personally Involved

*He's a rich mine of Common Sense for those who live well, a personal bodyguard to the candid and sincere. He keeps his eye on all who live honestly, and pays special attention to his loyally committed ones.*

PROVERBS 2:7–8 MSG

Have you ever considered that God is personally involved in your life? He offers wisdom and discernment as you navigate the ins and outs of life, and He's there to protect you when you feel vulnerable.

Maybe you're facing an intimidating situation. Maybe you feel uncovered and unprotected. Maybe your trust muscle has atrophied in fear or you're feeling an overwhelming sense of hopelessness. Maybe you're unsure of the next right step or are being blamed for things you didn't do.

When you're honest with and faithful to God, it's like a personal invitation for Him to be a part of your life. And He pays special attention to those who crave His loving interaction.

. . . . . . . . . . . . . . . . . . . . . . . . . . . . . . . . . . . . . .

*Father, I want to have an awesome relationship with You.*
*Every day, help me say yes to You. In Jesus' name I pray. Amen.*

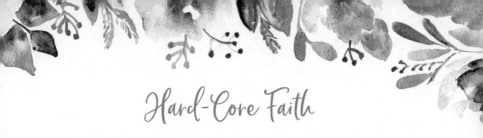

# Hard-Core Faith

*But those who trust in the Eternal One will regain their strength.*
*They will soar on wings as eagles. They will run—never winded,*
*never weary. They will walk—never tired, never faint.*
Isaiah 40:31 voice

When we have hard-core faith in the Lord it changes things. It means we believe who He says He is and surrender our worries and fears to Him. It means rather than lose our ever-lovin' mind in anger, we let the peace of Jesus take over. We hold on to Him instead of anything this world has to offer. And we don't give in to our painful circumstances or give up trying one more time. At every turn, we choose to trust Him for all we need.

That deliberate decision fills you with the faith you need to move forward. You'll be strengthened with endless motivation and perseverance for what you're experiencing. And your soul will be at peace.

* * * * * * * * * * * * * * * * * * * * * * * * * * * * * * * * * * * * *

*Father, help me trust You above anything the world can*
*offer me. In Jesus' name I pray. Amen.*

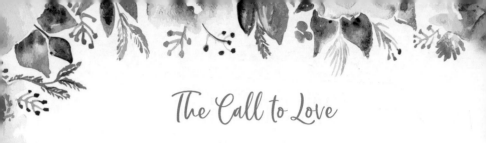

# The Call to Love

*Above all, constantly echo God's intense love for one another,*
*for love will be a canopy over a multitude of sins.*
1 PETER 4:8 TPT

Walking this verse out is all fine and dandy until we run across someone we don't want to love. It could be an ex-spouse or a nosy neighbor. It might be an abusive parent or a hateful coach. Maybe it's a friend who betrayed you, a group of women who rejected you, or a boss who belittled you. There are some people we just consider unlovable, and we find justification for holding on to offenses. And even though the pain is real and the hurt is formidable, God still wants us to love.

This doesn't mean being a doormat. Healthy boundaries are essential. But loving means you extend grace. And the only way you can is with Jesus, because in your own strength it's not sustainable. So, press into the One who is love and ask for His help.

*Father, I need Your help to love others.*
*Please soften my heart. In Jesus' name I pray. Amen.*

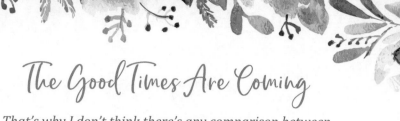

# The Good Times Are Coming

*That's why I don't think there's any comparison between the present hard times and the coming good times.*

ROMANS 8:18 MSG

No matter what you are walking through right now, it's going to get better. Even with the overwhelming heartache you're facing, it's not forever. The pain may feel so heavy and the battle may be relentless, but easier times are coming. This may be the most intense season of hurt and regret, but it will not last.

It's important to keep a perspective of hope rather than give in to despair. Don't let the tide of misery steal your joy for one second. Life is all about ebbs and flows, ups and downs. It's a series of seasons full of hardship and comfort. But the good times are coming, so hold on.

. . . . . . . . . . . . . . . . . . . . . . . . . . . . . . . . . . . . . . .

*Father, help me have the right perspective about the messy times in life. I want to live with hope rather than give in to sadness. And I'll need Your help with that. In Jesus' name I pray. Amen.*

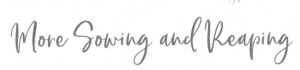

# More Sowing and Reaping

*Whoever pursues justice and treats others with kindness*
*discovers true life marked by integrity and respect.*
PROVERBS 21:21 VOICE

One of the most powerful concepts revealed throughout the Bible is the relationship between sowing and reaping. There is a real connection between how you choose to live today and the blessings and consequences that follow as a result.

Spend a moment thinking about the things you pursue with passion. Are they kingdom-focused, heart-friendly, relationship-building, grace-giving, love-sharing, kindness-extending, joy-creating, faith-empowering, and trust-encouraging pursuits? Or are they instead marked by self-centeredness?

Make no mistake, friend. What you choose to give will directly affect what you receive. That means it matters greatly how you live and love now because it affects what comes next. Be careful that what you are sowing in your pursuits is what you are hoping to reap from them in the future.

. . . . . . . . . . . . . . . . . . . . . . . . . . . . . . . . . . . .

*Father, give me the wisdom to pursue good and righteous things now*
*knowing it will influence my life in the future. And help me*
*choose wisely! In Jesus' name I pray. Amen.*

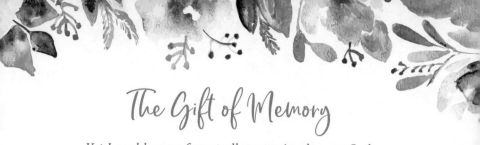

# The Gift of Memory

*Yet I could never forget all your miracles, my God,*
*as I remember all your wonders of old.*

PSALM 77:11 TPT

Memory is one of the greatest gifts we receive from God. It allows us to keep a Rolodex of reminders of where God intersected with our lives. It allows us to look back and remember God's goodness. It helps us trust Him for the road ahead. Memory of His faithfulness is vital to our faith because it awakens our courage while also settling our hearts.

Remember the times God showed up in the middle of your fear. Remember how He calmed anxiety about a diagnosis. Remember how He brought comfort despite betrayal or rejection. And never forget how God restored a relationship. There's powerful encouragement in your testimony.

Keep a journal of all He has done. There will come a time when you'll need a reminder that God is able.

. . . . . . . . . . . . . . . . . . . . . . . . . . . . . . . . . . . . . . . .

*Father, thank You for the gift of memory so I can recall*
*Your greatness in my life. In Jesus' name I pray. Amen.*

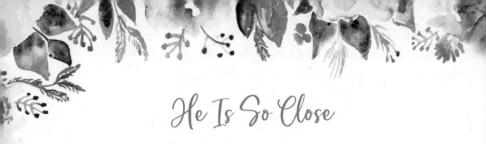

# He Is So Close

*The Lord is close to all whose hearts are crushed by pain,*
*and he is always ready to restore the repentant one.*

PSALM 34:18 TPT

God sees you when you're hurting. He knows when your heart has been crushed. God is not only fully aware of the moments you feel rejected, betrayed, abandoned, broken, and forgotten. . .He is also right there with you. What's more, He promises to restore you.

The pain may not stop right away. There are many gold nuggets you can only learn from the deep pits of pain. But in the end, the Father will heal your hurt, restore your trust, open your eyes, give you hope, reveal the truth, and show you ways He's made beauty from the ashes of your life.

Your friends and family will fall short. They'll let you down without knowing it. They'll offend you without meaning to. They'll try to rescue you, but they simply cannot. Trust that God can and will.

. . . . . . . . . . . . . . . . . . . . . . . . . . . . . . . . . . . . . . . . .

*Father, come close to me and restore me. In Jesus' name I pray. Amen.*

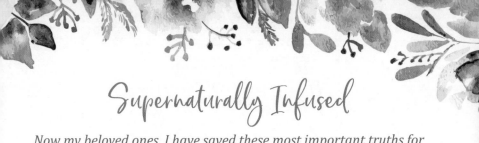

# Supernaturally Infused

*Now my beloved ones, I have saved these most important truths for last: Be supernaturally infused with strength through your life-union with the Lord Jesus. Stand victorious with the force of his explosive power flowing in and through you.*

EPHESIANS 6:10 TPT

It's not your job to find strength and courage on your own. You don't have to battle alone. Instead, you are supernaturally infused through your relationship with Jesus. How cool is that?

Honestly, the only hope we have to stand victoriously through life's storms is asking God for strength. He's the One who holds us up under adversity. He is why we have perseverance. Yes, it's His explosive power coursing through our veins that brings steadfastness.

So warrior, you're not beat. The world hasn't won. The situation won't ruin you. Don't you dare quit. Don't you dare give up in defeat. Don't you hide in bed, playing the victim. Instead, cry out for God to infuse you with His strength.

*Father, it's Your strength that helps me overcome and conquer. Thank You! In Jesus' name I pray. Amen.*

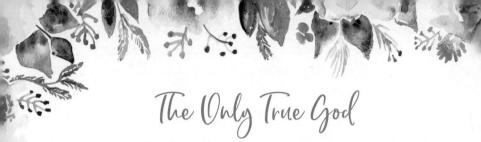

# The Only True God

*Know now then that the LORD your God is the only true God! He is the faithful God, who keeps the covenant and proves loyal to everyone who loves him and keeps his commands—even to the thousandth generation!*

DEUTERONOMY 7:9 CEB

Moses wanted us to know—without any doubt—that God in heaven is the only God. He is the true and faithful God, keeping His agreement of love with His children for a thousand lifetimes. That's epic.

Why do you think this truth needed to be stated so clearly? Maybe it's because people are quick to point to other religions and their gods as the way, but they're wrong. Maybe it's because there are idols we worship, and they steal our hearts away from Him. Maybe it's because God is a jealous God and He wants to captivate our hearts.

Make sure you worship the Lord, keeping His commands. Love Him with all your heart. And tell Him you do.

. . . . . . . . . . . . . . . . . . . . . . . . . . . . . . . . . .

*Father, You're the only true God. And I love You!*
*In Jesus' name I pray. Amen.*

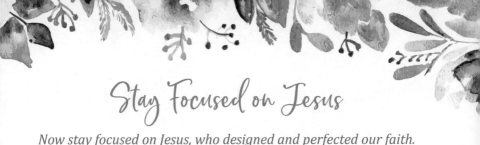

# Stay Focused on Jesus

*Now stay focused on Jesus, who designed and perfected our faith.*
*He endured the cross and ignored the shame of that death because*
*He focused on the joy that was set before Him; and now He*
*is seated beside God on the throne, a place of honor.*
HEBREWS 12:2 VOICE

In all you do, keep your focus on Jesus. He is a steadying force in your life because He knows what you're up against. He understands your struggles because He lived as a man and walked through messy situations just like you. He's experienced every human emotion. And Jesus promises to help you when you ask.

Don't focus on the confusing diagnosis, the rising bills, the rebellious child, the divorce papers, the looming deadline, the hurtful words, the uncertain future, the chaotic details, or the left turn your life just took. Focus on Him, sharing everything surrounding your fears, and know He will strengthen you to take the next right step.

*Father, give me wisdom to keep my eyes and heart*
*turned toward Jesus. In His name I pray. Amen.*

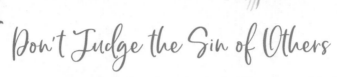

# Don't Judge the Sin of Others

*For we all have sinned and are in need of the glory of God.*
ROMANS 3:23 TPT

Everyone who lives and breathes on planet Earth will make poor choices and bad decisions. No one is exempt from temptations that lead to sinful actions. The problem is that we often compare our sin to their sin and decide we're better.

Don't judge someone because they sin differently than you. It's easy to look at their faults and feel superior because you've decided your offense isn't as grievous, but it's not your call to make. It's not your job. And it gives you a false sense of pride.

We can be concerned when we see people making bad choices. We can ask God for opportunities to come alongside them. And we can earn the right to speak into someone's life. But we cannot sit in the judgment seat. That seat is already taken.

. . . . . . . . . . . . . . . . . . . . . . . . . . . . . . . . . . . . . .

*Father, I confess my judgmental spirit. Help me remember that You are God and I am not. In Jesus' name I pray. Amen.*

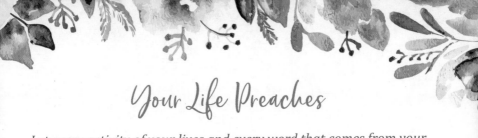

# Your Life Preaches

*Let every activity of your lives and every word that comes from your lips be drenched with the beauty of our Lord Jesus, the Anointed One. And bring your constant praise to God the Father because of what Christ has done for you!*

COLOSSIANS 3:17 TPT

Sometimes it's frustrating that God's commands are hard to live out. Rarely does He ask us to do easy things—things that are effortless or in our comfort zone. Instead, we're challenged to live drastically different than the world. God wants our lives to point to Him. He asks us to be His ambassadors on earth.

This command is painstakingly difficult most of the time. But regardless, let's be women who walk out faith well—women who encourage with words and affirm with actions—not because we want to impress, but because we want to hear "well done" when we meet Jesus face-to-face. What a privilege to let our lives preach.

. . . . . . . . . . . . . . . . . . . . . . . . . . . . . . . . . . . . . .

*Father, let my life point to Your grace and restorative powers. In Jesus' name I pray. Amen.*

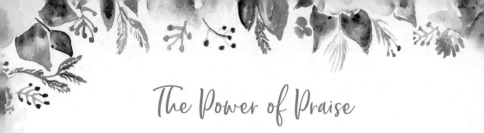

# The Power of Praise

*Clap your hands, all of you; raise your voices joyfully and loudly.*
*Give honor for the True God of the universe.*

PSALM 47:1 VOICE

It's easy to forget the power of our praise. Sometimes we focus our time with God on ranting and raving about the hardships we're facing. We may spend our prayer time asking Him for help, strength, wisdom, discernment, or peace. But our relationship with our heavenly Father isn't only about complaining and requesting. It's also very much about praising His name and thanking Him for His kindness.

What are you thankful for? Where has God been big? What beautiful outcomes and unexpected endings can you attribute to His power? Thank Him right now. Tell Him how much you love and appreciate Him. Tell God the impact of His help. Praise His name!

*Father, You're a good Dad. Help me not only see the times You work in my life, but also make the time to give You the praise You deserve. I'm so thankful for Your hand in my life. In Jesus' name I pray. Amen.*

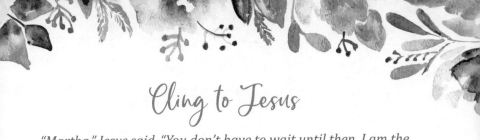

# Cling to Jesus

*"Martha," Jesus said, "You don't have to wait until then. I am the Resurrection, and I am Life Eternal. Anyone who clings to me in faith, even though he dies, will live forever."*

JOHN 11:25 TPT

This verse is one of the most powerful promises in the Word. It reveals the work of Jesus and how to spend eternity with Him and the Father. The key is clinging to Jesus.

What are the things you cling to for help and hope? Is it your marriage or the accomplishments of your kids? Is it your health? Maybe you're clinging to an addiction. What about an advanced degree or other academic achievement? It could be a friend or parent, or even a fail-proof process you learned from a book. Sweet one, there are no shortages of offerings from the world promising to fix us. But Jesus wants it to be Him.

. . . . . . . . . . . . . . . . . . . . . . . . . . . . . . . . . . . . . . . .

*Father, thank You for Jesus. Give me the courage to cling to Him over any worldly propositions. He is truly all I need. In Jesus' name I pray. Amen.*

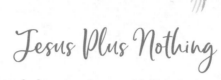

# Jesus Plus Nothing

*After he took the wine, Jesus said, "It's done. . .complete."*
*Bowing his head, he offered up his spirit.*
JOHN 19:30 MSG

Jesus' work on the cross was complete. It wasn't the beginning of something, nor did it follow up. It was a contained work. It was absolute. And Jesus' death fulfilled His purpose without fail. But sometimes we think we need to add to it.

When you ask Jesus to be your Savior, inviting Him into your life, it's a done deal. It's by faith in Him that you're saved. Be careful you don't buy into the belief that your actions factor into your salvation. Living right with God is important, but it's not part of the salvation equation. Your eternity in heaven is secured by Jesus plus nothing. Let your soul rest in that truth, and live in the freedom it provides!

. . . . . . . . . . . . . . . . . . . . . . . . . . . . . . . . . . . . . .

*Father, I am grateful that my eternity with You is not based on*
*my actions, because I am so imperfect. I'm thankful for Jesus'*
*complete work on the cross. In His name I pray. Amen.*

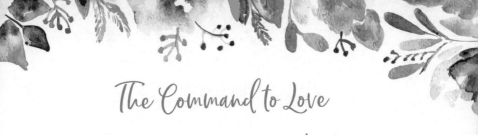

# The Command to Love

*"So I give you now a new commandment:*
*Love each other just as much as I have loved you."*
JOHN 13:34 TPT

This may be the hardest command next to forgiveness. Amen? It's easy to love when those around us are lovable, but it's a completely different story when people are hateful, bitter, opinionated, graceless, or taxing. We don't want to love others because they've hurt us.

But this command doesn't come with conditions. We can't opt out. We're either all-in or not. Of course, we can set healthy boundaries with toxic people, but we cannot hate them. So, choose to love the unlovable. Pray for them. Be kind. Be generous. Even with boundaries in place, speak of them and to them without hate.

Let us be known as women who love well. . .not perfectly, but with purpose.

. . . . . . . . . . . . . . . . . . . . . . . . . . . . . . . . . . .

*Father, I confess this is so hard for me. There are people I don't*
*consider lovable because of things they've done. Would You*
*soften my heart so I can release hurt and show*
*kindness? In Jesus' name I pray. Amen.*

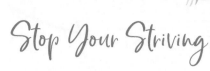

# Stop Your Striving

*Surrender your anxiety! Be silent and stop your striving and you will see that I am God. I am the God above all the nations, and I will be exalted throughout the whole earth.*

PSALM 46:10 TPT

The problem is that while we may know God is God, so often we act like we are. We grab hold of the reins of our lives and try to manipulate and control everything and everyone around us. We make decisions on our own without consulting our heavenly Father. And rather than submit to Him, we go at it alone. We work, work, work in our own strength.

God's desire for us is clear. Give Him our worries, quiet our anxious hearts, and let Him work toward the solution. When we choose this, peace overtakes us. We're comforted. We find rest. And choosing to cease striving gives us the ability to recognize our position in relation to His. We are letting God be God.

*Father, forgive me for playing god in my life.
I surrender it all to You. In Jesus' name I pray. Amen.*

# Joy Will Come from Your Tears

*Those who walk the fields to sow, casting their seed in tears,*
*will one day tread those same long rows, amazed by what's appeared.*
PSALM 126:5 VOICE

For many of us, this verse provides deep comfort to our troubled souls. Maybe you've been walking through a season of heartache that's left you weary and hopeless. It's been a time of second-guessing the situation and wondering where God is. Maybe you've emptied yourself of tears only to find a fresh batch the next day. But friend, God sees you.

Every tear that's spilled from your eyes has been seen by your Father. None of your pain has gone unnoticed. And He loves you so much that He makes you a promise that no one else can touch. He promises to bring joy from your pain. You will rise again.

. . . . . . . . . . . . . . . . . . . . . . . . . . . . . . . . . . . . . . . . .

*Father, my heart is broken and I feel hopeless. I cannot stop crying.*
*Please comfort me and remind me that I'm seen and that You're*
*a God who restores. In Jesus' name I pray. Amen.*

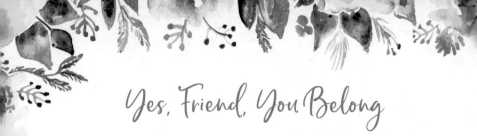

# Yes, Friend, You Belong

*And you are among the chosen ones who received the
call to belong to Jesus, the Anointed One.*

ROMANS 1:6 TPT

We all battle feelings of rejection. We did make it through middle school and high school, right? Every single one of us can remember times when we felt left out or overlooked. We didn't make the team, get the job, receive the invite, or get asked to homecoming. It's a common thread that weaves its way through every woman's heart. None of us are immune.

Maybe that's why God included this power-packed verse in His Word. This is the antidote to feeling rejected because it reminds us that we were handpicked—chosen by God Himself. He wanted you, friend. He saw immeasurable worth and value in who you are. And He just couldn't image a world (and an eternity) without you in it. Embrace the truth that you're needed and necessary.

* * * * * * * * * * * * * * * * * * * * * * * * * * * * * * * * * * * * * * * *

*Father, thank You for choosing me. Sometimes I need
a reminder that I belong. In Jesus' name I pray. Amen.*

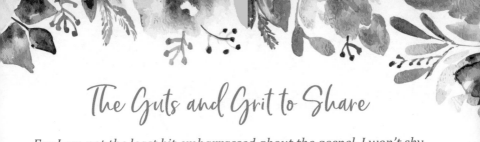

# The Guts and Grit to Share

*For I am not the least bit embarrassed about the gospel. I won't shy
away from it, because it is God's power to save every person
who believes: first the Jew, and then the non-Jew.*

ROMANS 1:16 VOICE

Let's face it. Today's world isn't as tolerant as in years past. Wouldn't
you agree? It seems like everyone is offended and angry. Gone are the
days when we could have differing opinions and still be friends. The
current mentality is "My way or the highway." And it's left us fearful
of boldly sharing our faith because we don't want the backlash that
may come with it.

But if we hold the Gospel tight for fear of embarrassment, how will
God's transformational truth reach the world? We don't have to yell
from the street corner or make a spectacle, but we can muster the guts
and grit to share our faith when God opens the door of opportunity.

*Father, I'm not ashamed. And I will speak of Your goodness
when the opportunity arises. In Jesus' name I pray. Amen.*

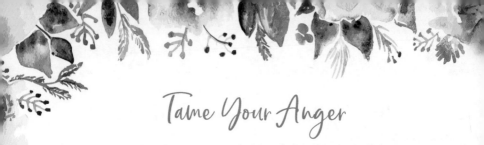

# Tame Your Anger

*Respond gently when you are confronted and you'll defuse the rage of another. Responding with sharp, cutting words will only make it worse. Don't you know that being angry can ruin the testimony of even the wisest of men?*

PROVERBS 15:1 TPT

It isn't easy to respond gently when someone rages against you. It takes maturity to stay calm when attacked. And it takes spending time with Jesus to learn to hold your tongue, especially because lashing out is often our default.

But remember that others are watching how you live your life. And because they know you love the Lord, they're watching your responses to life's ups and downs extra close. If you're preaching God's love one day and screaming in anger the next, it is confusing to those trying to figure this God thing out. It's not that you have to live perfectly, but you do need a passion to live with faith-filled purpose.

. . . . . . . . . . . . . . . . . . . . . . . . . . . . . . . . . . . . . . .

*Father, help me respond to others with maturity so my life points them to You. In Jesus' name I pray. Amen.*

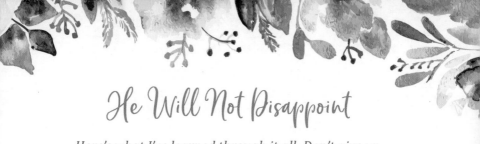

# He Will Not Disappoint

*Here's what I've learned through it all: Don't give up,*
*don't be impatient; be entwined as one with the Lord.*
*Be brave and courageous, and never lose hope. Yes,*
*keep on waiting—for he will never disappoint you!*
PSALM 27:14 TPT

Isn't waiting hard? Honestly, our society makes it so we don't have to wait for much of anything. Call-ahead seating, mobile ordering, self-checkout, and next-day delivery. . .this kind of treatment has trained us to be impatient. We've learned that waiting is inconvenient and wasteful. We want things now.

But God promises that if you have patience and persevere, good things will come to you—His good things. It may take all you've got to wait. You may have to ask God for peace through it. It may take every bit of courage you can muster not to take action yourself. But the Lord promises He will not disappoint!

*Father, I confess I'm horribly impatient these days.*
*I've fallen prey to the "I want it now" mentality. Help me be*
*tolerant of the wait. In Jesus' name I pray. Amen.*

# Taking Thoughts Captive

*We are demolishing arguments and ideas, every high-and-mighty*
*philosophy that pits itself against the knowledge of the one true*
*God. We are taking prisoners of every thought, every emotion,*
*and subduing them into obedience to the Anointed One.*
2 CORINTHIANS 10:5 VOICE

Many of us grew up knowing this verse. We had Sunday school teachers, small-group leaders, parents, and grandparents reminding us of the value of taking all thoughts captive. We've probably even heeded their advice from time to time with great results.

But this kind of discipline requires us to guard our thoughts on the regular. We have to be quick to grab truth and release lies. And every time fear or insecurity creeps in and whispers deceitfulness, we must choose to give it to God. Doing so will keep us in peace and living with confidence. And isn't that the best?

. . . . . . . . . . . . . . . . . . . . . . . . . . . . . . . . . . . . . . . . .

*Father, I only want truth to infiltrate my thoughts. Please give me*
*discernment to see lies, and wisdom to give them*
*to You. In Jesus' name I pray. Amen.*

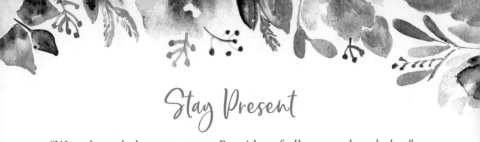

# Stay Present

*"We acknowledge you as our Provider of all we need each day."*
MATTHEW 6:11 TPT

As women, we're usually planners. We look ahead at what is and what may be. But this keeps us from being present in today. What's more, it scares us. Every time we turn our focus from the here and now to the future, we risk fear.

One of the Enemy's tactics is for us to look down the road and see nothing but horrible outcomes. Doing that usually leaves us anxious and overwhelmed, sometimes feeling helpless and hopeless. It stirs up all sorts of fears and worries, few of which ever come to pass. But when we instead focus on today and appreciate God's provision, we can find peace.

Keep your mind from the what-ifs of tomorrow. Focus your time and energy on today's joys and challenges. And hold steady against anyone or anything that tries to pull you out of the present.

. . . . . . . . . . . . . . . . . . . . . . . . . . . . . . . . . . . . . . . . .

*Father, You are my Provider, and I will stay*
*present with You! In Jesus' name I pray. Amen.*

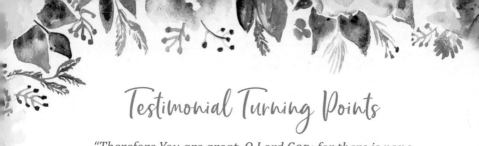

# Testimonial Turning Points

*"Therefore You are great, O Lord GOD; for there is none like You, and there is no God besides You, according to all that we have heard with our ears."*
2 SAMUEL 7:22 AMP

The power of testimony helped solidify Israel's understanding of who God is. The stories of healing, the stories of miracles, the recounting of God's deliverance and provision—these were all turning points for their belief. What a powerful reminder that when we share our God moments with others, it can encourage their faith in miraculous ways we may never have imagined.

Can you remember hearing how God moved mountains in someone's life, and their story gave you courage? Maybe it gave you strength for the battle or reminded you that God is in control so you don't have to hold it all together. Your faith grows by hearing others' stories of faith. Never miss an opportunity to listen or share His goodness!

*Father, thank You that testimonies can be turning points for us. In Jesus' name I pray. Amen.*

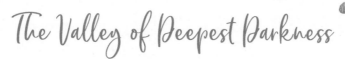

# The Valley of Deepest Darkness

*Lord, even when your path takes me through the valley of deepest darkness, fear will never conquer me, for you already have! You remain close to me and lead me through it all the way. Your authority is my strength and my peace. The comfort of your love takes away my fear. I'll never be lonely, for you are near.*

PSALM 23:4 TPT

Sometimes the paths God has chosen for us take us through the darkest of places. His choices are not meant to hurt us or take us out. Instead, He uses the valleys as learning opportunities to deepen our faith in Him. They're where God exposes places we need healing. And it's in these valleys we often feel closest to Him.

He's there to lead and strengthen. He brings peace. He comforts with His loving-kindness. And that love will cast out fear. He's got you.

* * *

*Father, help me trust You in the valleys rather than be afraid. I know You will be with me until I feel the sun on my face again. In Jesus' name I pray. Amen.*

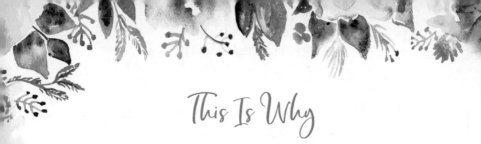

# This Is Why

*If your faith remains strong, even while surrounded by life's difficulties, you will continue to experience the untold blessings of God! True happiness comes as you pass the test with faith, and receive the victorious crown of life promised to every lover of God!*

JAMES 1:12 TPT

This promise is why you don't walk away when your marriage gets hard. It's why you don't give up when your kids act out. This promise is the reason you don't give in when you feel weak in the battle, or toss in the towel when you're scared to try again. This is why you choose not to crawl in a hole when the struggle feels endless.

Sister, God sees your decision to stay present. He knows there's a cost for persevering through the trials you face. And that's why He promises to bless you because of it.

. . . . . . . . . . . . . . . . . . . . . . . . . . . . . . . . . . . . . . . . . . .

*Father, please give me the strength I need to push through this hard season. I want to pass this test with faith in You so I can experience the untold blessings You promise. In Jesus' name I pray. Amen.*

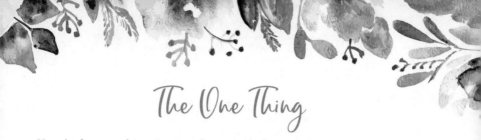

# The One Thing

*Here's the one thing I crave from God, the one thing I seek above all else: I want the privilege of living with him every moment in his house, finding the sweet loveliness of his face, filled with awe, delighting in his glory and grace. I want to live my life so close to him that he takes pleasure in my every prayer.*

PSALM 27:4 TPT

What's the one thing you want the most in this life? A fulfilling marriage or healthy children? A certain jean size or number on the scale? Recognition, riches, or fame? Deeper friendships or healing for a health condition?

Instead of anything the world offers, the psalmist wanted community with God. His heart was full of hope to be as close to Him as possible. He wanted to see His face, experience His glory, and live in such a way that even his prayers delighted God. What a beautiful goal that we can follow!

*Father, the one thing I crave above all else is You. In Jesus' name I pray. Amen.*

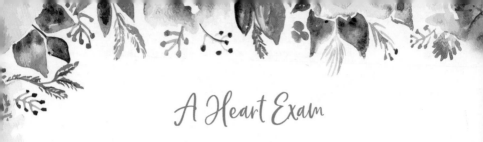

# A Heart Exam

*God, I invite your searching gaze into my heart. Examine me through and through; find out everything that may be hidden within me. Put me to the test and sift through all my anxious cares.*

PSALM 139:23 TPT

What would God find in your heart if He examined it? Is there unforgiveness tucked in there? Is it filled with anger? Are there fears and insecurities? Is there unhealed trauma? Asking God to search the depths of your heart is risky, but He is gentle and loving.

The truth is, God already knows what's there. He knows you better than you know yourself. So it would seem that inviting God to take a peek is more for you than for Him. It's a vulnerable act—one that requires epic levels of trust. And maybe this act of faith deepens your relationship in ways nothing else can. Friend, trust Him enough to invite Him in, and delight in the results.

* * *

*Father, search my heart. And let that act of trust build my faith even more. In Jesus' name I pray. Amen.*

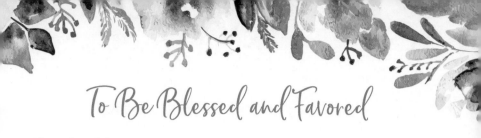

# To Be Blessed and Favored

*Blessed and favored by God are those who keep His testimonies, and who [consistently] seek Him and long for Him with all their heart.*

PSALM 119:2 AMP

God's hope and desire is to bless His children. His blessing and favor give us power and direction to live a righteous life. We learn to depend on and trust Him. And it's the Holy Spirit that gives us the ability to live out and love God's commands this way. It's His influence that helps us know what is wise and right and good.

What are the ways He's already blessing and favoring you? And what are some changes you could make today that would help you keep His commands and walk a more faithful path in life?

. . . . . . . . . . . . . . . . . . . . . . . . . . . . . . . . . . . . . . . . . .

*Father, thank You for the gift of blessing and favor. And thank You for the Holy Spirit to help guide me as I seek a more righteous life. I want my words and actions to delight You in every way! In Jesus' name I pray. Amen.*

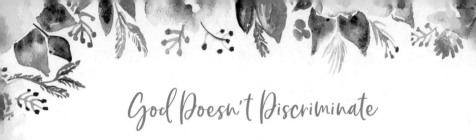

# God Doesn't Discriminate

*And it shall be that whoever shall call upon the name of the Lord*
*[invoking, adoring, and worshiping the Lord—Christ] shall be saved.*

ACTS 2:21 AMPC

God doesn't discriminate. It doesn't matter to Him what political party
you affiliate with. He doesn't care what side of the trendy social issue
you stand on. If you join the next movement or not, it doesn't sway His
opinion of you. Your past choices or current season of sinning aren't
factors in how much He loves you. And neither is your marital status,
education, state of residence, skin color, pants size, financial situation,
or age. God says *whoever* calls is saved. What a beautiful promise.

And since God doesn't discriminate, let's not either. Let's purpose
to love everyone—even those we disagree with.

* * * * * * * * * * * * * * * * * * * * * * * * * * * * * * * * * * *

*Father, what a big heart You have to allow us to be so diversified*
*without letting that affect how You feel. Your love isn't dependent;*
*it's unconditional. And Father, thank You for saving me when*
*I called Your name. In Jesus' name I pray. Amen.*

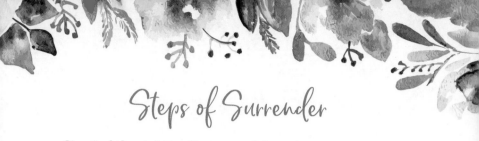

# Steps of Surrender

*Give God the right to direct your life, and as you trust him
along the way you'll find he pulled it off perfectly!*
PSALM 37:5 TPT

When life gets messy, trusting God is a choice. And sometimes it's a hard choice to make. It's scary to let go of the reins and trust an unseen God to direct our lives. We worry He'll miss something or be distracted by another more pressing situation. And so we end up vacillating between controlling the situation and surrendering it to the Lord.

Let this verse encourage you to trust God with what you're walking through. His ways are perfect, and He is capable of multitasking. And every time you take a step of surrender and He proves Himself faithful, it helps build your belief that He is a can-do kind of God who wants to and will!

. . . . . . . . . . . . . . . . . . . . . . . . . . . . . . . . . . . . . . . . .

*Father, help me find the courage and confidence in You to
take those small steps of surrender. I want to trust
You wholeheartedly! In Jesus' name I pray. Amen.*

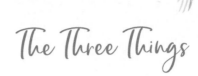

# The Three Things

*But for right now, until that completeness, we have three things*
*to do to lead us toward that consummation: Trust steadily*
*in God, hope unswervingly, love extravagantly.*
*And the best of the three is love.*

1 CORINTHIANS 13:13 MSG

Until we see Jesus face-to-face, there are three ways prescribed for us to live out our days. We're to trust God without fail, hold on to hope no matter what, and love in excess. While it may be easy to say we'll do it and make plans to do it, these three things take guts and grit to walk out in real time. They don't always come easily, and living this way takes loads of prayer and buckets full of determination. True, we can't perfect them, but we can be purposeful in our pursuit. And when we are, it's beautiful for us, God, and others.

* * * * * * * * * * * * * * * * * * * * * * * * * * * * * * * * * * * * * *

*Father, these three things—trust, hope, and love—aren't easy to*
*muster. Help me be purposeful so they can be part of my life*
*in significant ways. In Jesus' name I pray. Amen.*

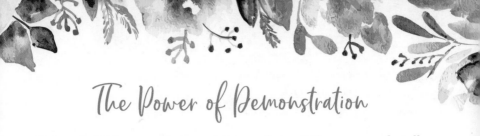

# The Power of Demonstration

*Beloved children, our love can't be an abstract theory we only talk about, but a way of life demonstrated through our loving deeds.*

1 JOHN 3:18 TPT

The world would be a better place if everyone lived this verse out. John reminded believers of the power of demonstration because the truth is that showing always means more than telling. Doing is more influential than promising, every time. And when you show people you love them rather than just telling them, your effort goes the extra mile. Without fail, action over the spoken word always wins.

Who in your life needs to see your love for them? How do they receive love best? Acts of service? Quality time? Physical touch? A thoughtful gift? Make time this week to be purposeful in demonstrating your feelings toward those you love. They need it.

* * * * * * * * * * * * * * * * * * * * * * * * * * * * * * * * * * *

*Father, help me be creative and purposeful in showing love to my friends and family. I don't want anyone to doubt my feelings toward them. In Jesus' name I pray. Amen.*

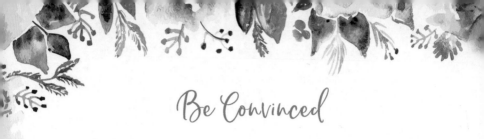

# Be Convinced

*I'm absolutely convinced that nothing—nothing living or dead,
angelic or demonic, today or tomorrow, high or low, thinkable or
unthinkable—absolutely nothing can get between us and God's
love because of the way that Jesus our Master has embraced us.*
ROMANS 8:38–39 MSG

There are a million things that can wreak havoc on the love we feel
toward others. Betrayal from a spouse. Continual fighting within a family.
Lack of gratitude. Abusive and reckless words. Dismissive attitudes.
Control and manipulation. Broken promises. Rejection. Abandonment.
Love here is unstable and imperfect.

But God's love for you is unchanging. He literally cannot love you
any more or any less than He does right now—and always has. Nothing
you've done or will do has the power to affect how much He adores you,
friend. So while the world may be fickle, remember that God is faithful.

*Father, I am convinced of Your love for me. I don't know how You love
so perfectly, but I sure am glad You do! In Jesus' name I pray. Amen.*

# Are You Ready for Something New?

*Watch closely: I am preparing something new; it's happening now, even as I speak, and you're about to see it. I am preparing a way through the desert; waters will flow where there had been none.*

ISAIAH 43:19 VOICE

Chances are there's a situation you're in right now where you're ready for a breakthrough. It could be health related or a difficult season at your job. You may have toddlers teething or be dealing with the roller coaster of teenage emotions. Maybe you're single and ready for marriage, or maybe your marriage has hit hard times. At some point we all crave a change—a new and fresh change from where we've been.

You can trust that God already has something new in the works. He doesn't leave you where you are for long, and His timing for unveiling a new direction is flawless. Are you desperate for God to do a new thing? Watch closely. It's coming.

* * * * * * * * * * * * * * * * * * * * * * * * * * * * * * * * * * * * * * * *

*Father, I am ready for a fresh start. And I trust Your plans for me! In Jesus' name I pray. Amen.*

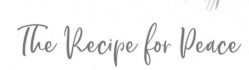

# The Recipe for Peace

*Don't shuffle along, eyes to the ground, absorbed with the things right in front of you. Look up, and be alert to what is going on around Christ—that's where the action is. See things from his perspective.*

COLOSSIANS 3:2 MSG

The recipe for peace is Jesus. That means when the going gets tough, we turn to Him. We pray, asking for harmony, clarity, understanding, wisdom, discernment, and hope. He has the power to comfort our hearts so they don't race toward horrible outcomes. It's easy to get lost in stress, and rather than look to Him for understanding, we get caught up in the what-ifs. And nothing takes us out of peace faster than what-ifs.

How do you usually find peace apart from Jesus? How do you settle your anxious heart? No matter what it is, the peace that comes from Jesus is always better.

*Father, I want the peace You offer to be ever present in my life. Thank You for giving it so freely. In Jesus' name I pray. Amen.*

# Love Matters

*What if I speak in the most elegant languages of people or in the
exotic languages of the heavenly messengers, but I live without
love? Well then, anything I say is like the clanging
of brass or a crashing cymbal.*

1 Corinthians 13:1 voice

This verse is calling you higher. It's talking about the importance of
living with authenticity and letting love rule in your heart. Paul's point
is simple and clear. It doesn't matter how much money you make or
how well known your family name is in town. It doesn't matter how
much schooling you've gone through or how fancy your wardrobe is.
You may have vacation homes or a personal chef. Without kindness
and love, it's pointless.

Love matters and should be of the highest value in your life. The
things you collect in life will fade away, but the way you choose to love
others has the potential for far-reaching results.

· · · · · · · · · · · · · · · · · · · · · · · · · · · · · · · · · · · · ·

*Father, help love reign in my heart so it manifests in my life.
In Jesus' name I pray. Amen.*

# The Responsibility to Shine Brightly

*"So don't hide your light! Let it shine brightly before others, so that the commendable things you do will shine as light upon them, and then they will give their praise to your Father in heaven."*

MATTHEW 5:16 TPT

If you love Jesus and have invited Him to be your personal Savior, there is a beautiful light inside you that is meant for the world to see. They see it through your transformed life. When you are kind to a stranger, helpful to a neighbor, or thoughtful toward a teacher, God is glorified. When you volunteer your time, pray with a friend, show up for a single mom, or lead a Bible study, others notice your generosity.

The point of your life is for it to point to your Father. That's the power of the light within you—a light that shines because of Jesus.

*Father, I don't always do good and right things that point to Your goodness. Help me be more aware of shining my light so others praise Your name. In Jesus' name I pray. Amen.*

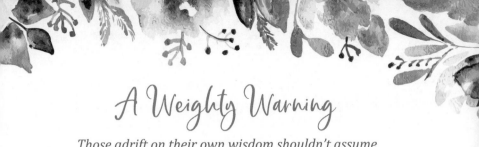

# A Weighty Warning

*Those adrift on their own wisdom shouldn't assume*
*the Lord will rescue them or bring them anything.*

JAMES 1:7 VOICE

What a weighty warning. When we ignore God's will and ways and do what we want instead, there's a good chance we'll be left to walk out the natural consequences of that decision. We can't assume that God will course-correct our stubbornness and blatant disobedience. He can and He has before, but sometimes God leaves us to weather the aftermath on our own. It's in those times He helps us see the error of our ways as well as His hope for us to make better choices next time.

God's wisdom is available to you at any moment. It's a promise. He knows that life is full of choices and that sometimes it's hard to know what's best, but God will make you discerning and wise when you ask for His help.

. . . . . . . . . . . . . . . . . . . . . . . . . . . . . . . . . .

*Father, please give me wisdom to know Your will for me.*
*And give me courage to choose it. In Jesus' name I pray. Amen.*

# The Powerful Weapon of Gratitude

*Every good gift, every perfect gift, comes from above. These gifts come down from the Father, the creator of the heavenly lights, in whose character there is no change at all.*

JAMES 1:17 CEB

When you recognize the role God has played in your life and all the times He's shown up at just the right moment, it should overwhelm you. Remembering His loving intervention when things looked hopeless should undo you. Recounting the ways God took care of your heart, the crooked paths He straightened, and the Enemy's plans He thwarted should have you on your knees with deep appreciation.

Gratitude is a powerful weapon because it breeds contentment. We realize we have enough—we have everything because of God. And it keeps us focused on His goodness rather than our present mess. Since He always has before, we know we can trust Him to be there for us again.

*Father, my heart is so full of gratitude for You. Thank You for every good and perfect gift! In Jesus' name I pray. Amen.*

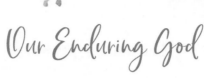

# Our Enduring God

*How enduring is God's loyal love;*
*the Eternal has inexhaustible compassion.*
LAMENTATIONS 3:22 VOICE

Can you think of times when you needed a do-over? Maybe you spoke out of turn and hurt someone's feelings. Maybe you shared a secret you promised not to share. Maybe you had a moral failure—one you never thought was possible. Or maybe you made a risky choice that didn't pan out the way you'd hoped. We all have times when we royally mess up and wish for another chance to make things right.

But God doesn't hold mistakes over your head. When you mess up, you don't need to beg for a do-over. God doesn't keep score of your wrongs. And it's His loyal love and inexhaustible compassion for you that ensures you'll never have to worry about being abandoned by the One who created you. His love endures.

* * * * * * * * * * * * * * * * * * * * * * * * * * * * * * * * * * * * * * * * * *

*Father, I'm so thankful there's nothing I can do to wear You*
*out or exhaust You enough to make You walk away*
*from me. In Jesus' name I pray. Amen.*

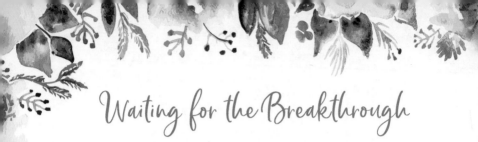

# Waiting for the Breakthrough

*This is why I wait upon you, expecting your*
*breakthrough, for your word brings me hope.*
PSALM 130:5 TPT

This is a gutsy move. It takes a venti-sized dose of courage to wait for the Lord to show up while a storm is brewing all around you. It takes grit to stand still until God unveils the next right step in the journey. It requires determined faith to believe He is aware of your struggles and diligently working to straighten the crooked path you're on. The Word of God provides insight and encouragement for these things. We can wait on the Lord because He is our hope.

Looking back, can you see times when your patience and trust paid off? Can you see situations where breakthrough came at the right moment? Friend, your God is trustworthy. He is working things out for your good. Ask for peace as you wait, and remember, breakthrough is right around the corner.

*Father, I will wait on You always because I know You will*
*come through in the end. In Jesus' name I pray. Amen.*

# What Does the Bible Say about It?

*Truth's shining light guides me in my choices and decisions;*
*the revelation of your word makes my pathway clear.*

PSALM 119:105 TPT

Ever wonder if what you think or what you want to do lines up with God's will? Or if what you feel He's asking of you is legit? What's more, do you sometimes question if it's even His voice you're hearing? These questions are common among believers. Why not see what the Bible has to say about it?

In every situation, there's a right way and a wrong way, but sometimes it's hard to tell the difference between the two. That's why we need God's voice more than the ideas and opinions of those we love. He has a plan already in place and knows the next right step to get you where you need to be. Ask God to use His Word to affirm and confirm.

. . . . . . . . . . . . . . . . . . . . . . . . . . . . . . . . . . . . . . . .

*Father, I want to choose wisely, but I need Your help. Would You guide my steps through Your words? In Jesus' name I pray. Amen.*

## Draw Closer

*Come close to the one true God, and He will draw close to you.*
*Wash your hands; you have dirtied them in sin. Cleanse your*
*heart, because your mind is split down the middle, your love*
*for God on one side and selfish pursuits on the other.*

JAMES 4:8 VOICE

Cling to God, sweet one. In hard times, draw close to Him. When grief feels almost unbearable, when it feels like your broken heart is going to explode, when your current season of sinning is tearing you apart, hold on to your Father. When sleep eludes you and guilt consumes you, cry out for His help. When you're drenched in shame and feelings of unworthiness because of the bad choices you've made, ask God to come closer.

With tear-stained cheeks and guttural cries, grab hold of the only One who can bring healing to your weary soul. He isn't angry with you. He won't ever reject you. And when you draw close to Him, He will be there every time.

. . . . . . . . . . . . . . . . . . . . . . . . . . . . . . . . . . . . . . . . . . . .

*Father, I need You. In Jesus' name I pray. Amen.*

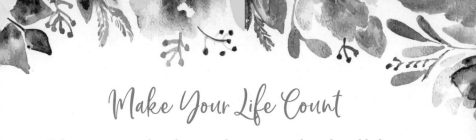

# Make Your Life Count

*Help us to remember that our days are numbered, and help us*
*to interpret our lives correctly. Set your wisdom deeply in*
*our hearts so that we may accept your correction.*
PSALM 90:12 TPT

It's important to remember that your one and only life here on planet Earth is short. It's a breath compared to eternity. And even if you live to be one hundred years old, time flies by quickly. The psalmist understood this truth and was resolved to make his life count. Let's choose to live the same way.

When you wake in the morning, ask God for the wisdom needed to live your best life that day. Be measured in your words and thoughtful with your time. Listen for God's guidance so you can follow His lead. Watch for open doors and closed doors, and ask for His discernment to know the difference. You're here for a reason, so make your life count!

* * * * * * * * * * * * * * * * * * * * * * * * * * * * * * * * * * * * *

*Father, I want to live out Your plan for me. Help me be wise*
*and purposeful every day. In Jesus' name I pray. Amen.*

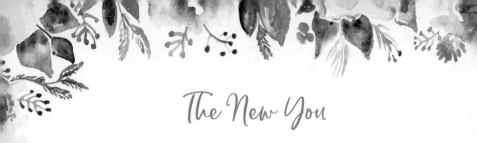

# The New You

*Therefore, if anyone is united with the Anointed One, that person is a new creation. The old life is gone—and see—a new life has begun!*
2 Corinthians 5:17 voice

There's something compelling about saying goodbye to old ways and hello to a new way of living. It's refreshing and empowering to make a change. Maybe it's a new, healthier eating plan. Maybe it's starting mornings with prayer instead of Instagram. It might be new friends who make better life choices. And while change isn't always easy or free of emotion, it does reset your heart. It refocuses your perspective. And it can straighten your backbone and resolve.

When you accepted Jesus as your Savior, you became new. He took the old you and spiffed it up, making you stronger and wiser and fueled by the Holy Spirit. With Him, you have the ability to live differently. It's not a call to perfection. It's a choice to be purposeful.

* * * * * * * * * * * * * * * * * * * * * * * * * * * * * * * * * * * * * *

*Father, thank You for making me new in You!*
*In Jesus' name I pray. Amen.*

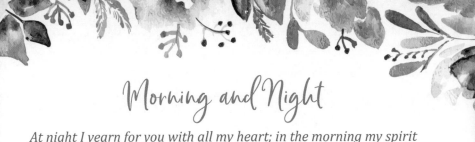

# Morning and Night

*At night I yearn for you with all my heart; in the morning my spirit reaches out to you. When you display your judgments on the earth, people learn the ways of righteousness.*

Isaiah 26:9 TPT

The writer's soul longed for God day and night. He loved the Lord with all his heart, and that love compelled him to pour into their relationship. He decided to make it a priority. And he knew that living right with God was his greatest desire.

How about you? What is your greatest desire? Where is your relationship with God in your list of priorities? Sister, you were created to be in a relationship with your heavenly Father. His desire is for you to covet time with Him. He wants to be the first thing you think of when you wake and the last thing on your mind as you fall asleep.

*Father, forgive me for not always showing You how important You are to me. I am going to change that! In Jesus' name I pray. Amen.*

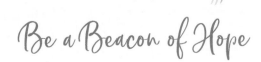

# Be a Beacon of Hope

*"Your lives light up the world. Let others see your light from a distance, for how can you hide a city that stands on a hilltop?"*
<small>MATTHEW 5:14 TPT</small>

Have you ever considered this? Because of Jesus in you, you're a light in a world that can often be dark. People are lost and broken and deeply in need of a Savior. God wants your life to reflect the light of His majesty so others can find hope and healing through Him.

It's both a privilege and a burden to make sure your words and actions point to God. He says you are light, and that's a beautifully difficult calling. But when you spend time with Him, your light shines. It's not because of you. It's because of Him. Your job is to live out that passion and purpose so your light for God is bright.

. . . . . . . . . . . . . . . . . . . . . . . . . . . . . . . . . . . . . . . .

*Father, thank You for making me a light! Help me remember that so I can be mindful to live and love well. In Jesus' name I pray. Amen.*

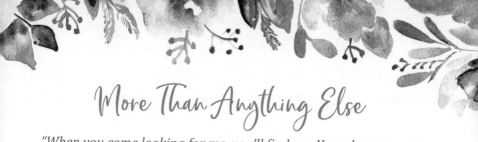

# More Than Anything Else

*"When you come looking for me, you'll find me. Yes, when you get serious about finding me and want it more than anything else, I'll make sure you won't be disappointed."*

JEREMIAH 29:13 MSG

We dabble, don't we? We want God to intervene when the going gets tough, but then we often set Him on a shelf when times are good. When everything that could go wrong does, we cry out for His help. But once the dust settles, back to the shelf He goes. God wants more than that from us and for us. He wants commitment to a relationship that doesn't ebb and flow with the tides of life.

God promises that when you truly dedicate yourself to Him, you won't be disappointed. In other words, the effort you'll expend to grow your relationship with Him will be worth it. There are benefits to it. Why not give it a try?

. . . . . . . . . . . . . . . . . . . . . . . . . . . . . . . . . . . . . .

*Father, forgive me for being inconsistent with You. Help me want You more than anything else. In Jesus' name I pray. Amen.*

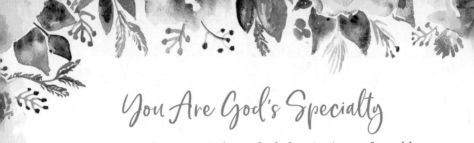

# You Are God's Specialty

*The Eternal One is good, a safe shelter in times of trouble.*
*He cares for those who search for protection in Him.*
NAHUM 1:7 VOICE

More than your best friend. . .more than your husband. . .more than your parents. . .more than your siblings. . .more than your kids—hold on to *God*. He is your safe shelter from anything life throws your way. He has the power to save, to heal, to redirect, to undo, to override, and to deliver you safely through the storm. There is nothing and nobody that can match His love and care for you!

Where are you feeling vulnerable? What's making you afraid? Listen, helping you is God's specialty. When you ask for His help, He takes your request seriously. He will always come through. And you can always trust Him to step in. Why? Because He is always good. He is your unwavering safe place, and nothing will stop Him from caring for you.

* * * * * * * * * * * * * * * * * * * * * * * * * * * * * * * * * * * * * * * *

*Father, I'm so grateful for Your care and concern.*
*In Jesus' name I pray. Amen.*

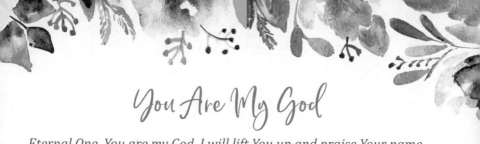

# You Are My God

*Eternal One, You are my God. I will lift You up and praise Your name.
Because You have made wonders marvelous and beautiful—
the most ancient designs holding strong and sure.*
ISAIAH 25:1 VOICE

Here's where we get tripped up. We start making other things our god—our savior. Rather than giving the Lord praise, we find satisfaction from overeating. We drink or shop to make us feel better. We praise images on social media and strive to be more like them. We put people on a pedestal and decide they're worthy of our worship. And sometimes we're prideful, thinking we have all the answers and control.

But God is the only God. He's the One who makes things beautiful and marvelous. He's the One whose wonders are noteworthy. It's Him, and Him alone. Be mindful of what you're worshipping, friend. Be aware of what gets your attention on the regular.

* * * * * * * * * * * * * * * * * * * * * * * * * * * * * * * * * * * * * * * * *

*Father, You are my God—now and always. I'm sorry I've put others
in Your place. I'm changing that! In Jesus' name I pray. Amen.*

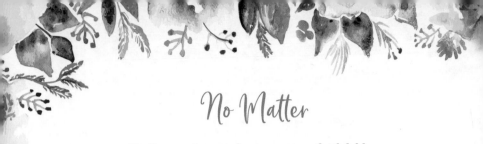

# No Matter

*My lips praise you because your faithful love
is better than life itself!*
PSALM 63:3 CEB

No matter the awards you were given at work or the degrees you earned. No matter how happy your marriage is or how well your child did in school. No matter what disease you overcame or how much money you've banked in retirement. No matter your personal achievements or the workout goals you're crushing. No matter what amazing things life has to offer, God's love bests them every time.

The high you feel from any earthly success or accomplishment is temporary. It's fleeting. It will only satisfy for a moment. But God's love for you is never-ending. It doesn't expire. It never falls flat. It can't be beat. And nothing can make it diminish. The Lord loves you fully, completely, and without fail. You can't earn it or lose it. Now that is worthy of praise!

*Father, I am in awe of how great Your love is for me!
Nothing earthly can even come close. In Jesus' name I pray. Amen.*

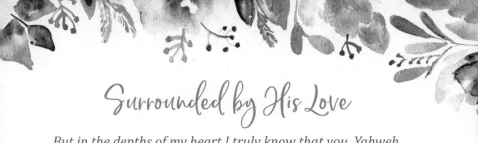

# Surrounded by His Love

*But in the depths of my heart I truly know that you, Yahweh,*
*have become my Shield; you take me and surround me with*
*yourself. Your glory covers me continually. You lift*
*high my head when I bow low in shame.*

PSALM 3:3 TPT

From every direction and angle, you're completely surrounded by God's love for you. Take a moment to see that image in your mind's eye. Notice there are no gaps in coverage. There isn't an opening He's missed. His love is all-encompassing and doesn't leave space for anything unwanted to challenge it. And this love for you is continuous. It is for always. And it cannot be usurped.

Remember this image when dark days threaten your joy. When lies try to infiltrate your heart and discourage you, visualize His love fully covering you. In those moments when you feel overwhelmed and afraid, see yourself surrounded by His glory. Sweet one, you're fully protected and engulfed by God's love for you.

* * * * * * * * * * * * * * * * * * * * * * * * * * * * * * * * * * * * *

*Father, I know You've got me. Thank You. In Jesus' name I pray. Amen.*

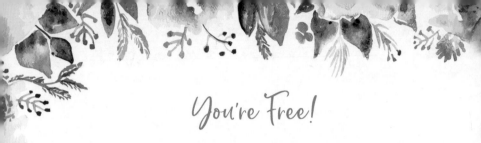

# You're Free!

*But now in a single victorious stroke of Life, all three—sin, guilt, death—are gone, the gift of our Master, Jesus Christ. Thank God!*
1 CORINTHIANS 15:57 MSG

Despite how scary the circumstances may look right now. Regardless of how overwhelming the situations before you may seem to be. No matter how many odds appear to be stacked against you. Because of Jesus Christ, you'll be victorious. You will come out ahead. You will win in the end. And you will stand in amazement as you look at all that God has done for you.

The truth is, He thought of everything. He knew the power that sin, guilt, and death would have over your heart and life, and it didn't sit well with your Father. So rather than leave it be, He sent His one and only Son to fix it. Jesus' death on the cross ensured your victory. And because of it, you are free!

. . . . . . . . . . . . . . . . . . . . . . . . . . . . . . . . . . .

*Father, thank You for victory through Christ!*
*What a relief that He made a way. In His name I pray. Amen.*

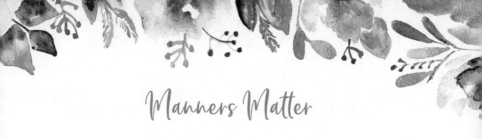

# Manners Matter

*"Now therefore, our God, we thank You,*
*and praise Your glorious name."*
1 CHRONICLES 29:13 AMP

You may ask, beg, and bargain with God for the things you need and want, but do you stop and thank Him? It's easy to rattle off an endless list of prayer requests, but are you giving credit to God for the answers? Are you recognizing His power in your life? Do you thank Him for the peace you wanted or the strength you needed? Have you stopped to acknowledge the ways He's shown up for you?

Just like you appreciate gratitude for things you've done to help others, it delights God's heart for you to express thanks too. It's good manners to say a heartfelt thank-You to your Father for His lavish kindness and demonstrative love. And we all know manners matter.

*Father, I wanted to say thank You for being so good to me.*
*I see Your hand in my life, and I know You're the reason*
*I have what I need. In Jesus' name I pray. Amen.*

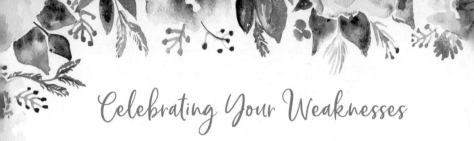

# Celebrating Your Weaknesses

*But he answered me, "My grace is always more than enough for you,*
*and my power finds its full expression through your weakness."*
*So I will celebrate my weaknesses, for when I'm weak I sense*
*more deeply the mighty power of Christ living in me.*
2 CORINTHIANS 12:9 TPT

Celebrating weaknesses goes against the world's thinking. Society tells you to be strong no matter what. It says to ignore anyone who says you *can't*. Rather than ask for help, you should dig deep inside for it. This kind of thinking leaves no room to be vulnerable about your limitations. You're supposed to grin and bear it. And while you may be struggling on the inside, no one would know it from the outside.

God sees weakness as an opportunity to demonstrate His power and might. Because when you're at the end of you and suddenly feel that surge of hope, strength, peace, or wisdom, no one can doubt His faithfulness.

* * * * * * * * * * * * * * * * * * * * * * * * * * * * * * * * * * * * * * *

*Father, I like the way You see things. Help me see*
*them Your way too. In Jesus' name I pray. Amen.*

# The Foundation of All Happiness

*All has been heard; the end of the matter is: Fear God [revere and worship Him, knowing that He is] and keep His commandments, for this is the whole of man [the full, original purpose of his creation, the object of God's providence, the root of character, the foundation of all happiness, the adjustment to all inharmonious circumstances and conditions under the sun] and the whole [duty] for every man.*

ECCLESIASTES 12:13 AMPC

We all want to be happy. We surround ourselves with people and things that make us feel content—that make us feel like we matter. We marry for happiness. We buy new clothes so we feel good in them. We decorate our homes because they're our happy place. We buy food that delights our senses and go on vacations that make us squeal with excitement. But these should never be the foundation of our happiness.

It's knowing God and keeping His commands that will give you true joy.

· · · · · · · · · · · · · · · · · · · · · · · · · · · · · · · · · · · · · ·

*Father, You make me happy. I love You! In Jesus' name I pray. Amen.*

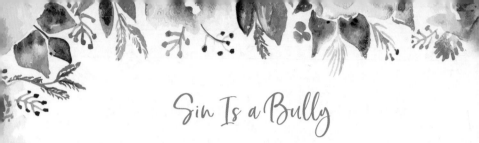

# Sin Is a Bully

*Sin can't tell you how to live. After all, you're not living under that old tyranny any longer. You're living in the freedom of God.*

ROMANS 6:14 MSG

Sin has a way of pulling you deeper into it because there's a payoff. Even if only for a moment, it makes you feel good. It offers a break from the pain or heartache. It's an escape from all that's wrong in your life. Sin promises you things, tricking you into doing it one more time. And at the same time, it discourages you by whispering, "You'll never break free, so why even try?"

But Jesus died on the cross for your freedom. He put the bully of sin in its rightful place and gave you the power to overcome it. Saying no is a tough choice to make, but if you ask God for help, you will have all you need to kick the bully to the curb.

. . . . . . . . . . . . . . . . . . . . . . . . . . . . . . . . . . . . . .

*Father, sin can't tell me how to live—because of Jesus.*
*Thank You for the reminder! In Jesus' name I pray. Amen.*

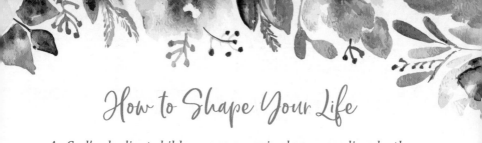

# How to Shape Your Life

*As God's obedient children, never again shape your lives by the desires that you followed when you didn't know better.*

1 PETER 1:14 TPT

Before we knew Jesus, our lives were shaped by bad choices, selfish desires, and living for all the wrong things. We didn't know any better, so we did what felt good and right without batting an eye. Our moral compass wasn't pointing to the Truth, so chances are it didn't factor into our decisions. But then we met Jesus.

Peter is challenging us with today's verse. He's telling us to be intentional with our lives, making sure our choices reflect a relationship with God. He's asking us to have eyes wide open to how we're living, and shaping our lives around the Lord. We may not have understood righteous living before Jesus, but we do now.

*Father, help me be obedient to Your will and ways. I want my life to reflect my relationship with You in everything I do. In Jesus' name I pray. Amen.*

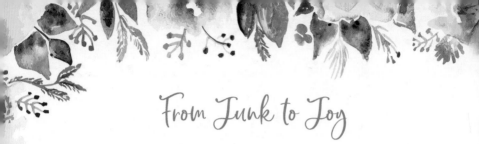

# From Junk to Joy

*His anger lasts for only a second, but his favor lasts a lifetime.*
*Weeping may stay all night, but by morning, joy!*
PSALM 30:5 CEB

Every day is a new day, which means it's a chance to start over fresh. You may have had an argument the night before, but the morning brings a new chance for reconciliation. There might have been tears of grief as you laid your head on the pillow, but God brings comfort as you open your eyes. Stress may have stolen sweet slumber, but He will drench you in His peace if you ask.

The encouragement here is that whatever you're going through won't last forever. Your situations and seasons can change overnight, and your heartache can become hope. Your circumstance can go from junk to joy in a moment's notice. So trust God with your struggles. His favor rests on you.

. . . . . . . . . . . . . . . . . . . . . . . . . . . . . . . . . . . . . .

*Father, I need to know things can get better. I feel overwhelmed by*
*the challenges I'm facing, and I'm losing hope. Please help*
*me. In Jesus' name I pray. Amen.*

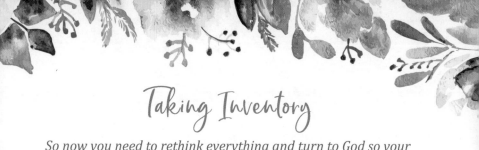

# Taking Inventory

*So now you need to rethink everything and turn to God so your*
*sins will be forgiven and a new day can dawn, days of*
*refreshing times flowing from the Lord.*
ACTS 3:19 VOICE

Maybe it's time you rethought some of your life choices. Taking inventory regularly helps you stay focused on living God's way rather than slipping back into old habits. It's not about condemnation. It's about allowing the Holy Spirit to gently turn your head and heart back to God. And it tells the Lord that you care about living your one and only life to glorify Him.

So ask yourself if there's anything you're watching or listening to that's offensive to God. Are your thoughts glorifying Him? Are you being intentional with your words, making sure you're not using them as weapons? Are you harboring unforgiveness or anger? Is there unchecked pride in your heart? Monitoring your faith walk will set you up for blessings!

*Father, my heart is to live my life glorifying You.*
*Please give me confidence to do it. In Jesus' name I pray. Amen.*

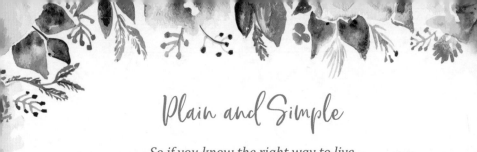

# Plain and Simple

*So if you know the right way to live
and ignore it, it is sin—plain and simple.*
JAMES 4:17 VOICE

It takes guts and grit to walk away from sinful living because it's often the most popular choice. Sin can be packed with worldly fun that's difficult to turn from. And standing up for what you know is right often strains relationships or ends them altogether. But your relationship with the Lord should be your highest priority. That often means you'll have to make hard decisions—ones that also come with blessings.

The Holy Spirit in you will ensure you know the right way to live, whether it's a gut feeling or your intuition. God won't hide His hopes for your life from you. They will be plain and simple. The more you spend time with Him, the clearer you'll hear Him. And that clarity will be your guide to living with purpose and passion.

*Father, let me hear You so I'll know Your will
for my life. In Jesus' name I pray. Amen.*

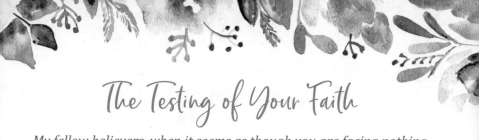

# The Testing of Your Faith

*My fellow believers, when it seems as though you are facing nothing*
*but difficulties see it as an invaluable opportunity to experience the*
*greatest joy that you can! For you know that when your faith is*
*tested it stirs up power within you to endure all things.*
JAMES 1:2–3 TPT

Unless we face hard times, how will we mature? How will we learn to trust God if life's a cakewalk? Without pitfalls and heartaches, how are we supposed to learn endurance? Where's the incentive to change or grow when everything's predictable? God uses those tough times for His purpose. They test our faith through a choice. Will we trust God or take control?

When we activate faith and lean into our Father through the storms, we come out stronger. And joy comes from knowing we stood the test and chose to believe God's power and might.

. . . . . . . . . . . . . . . . . . . . . . . . . . . . . . . . . . . . . . . . .

*Father, I appreciate the way You see things. Who knew joy*
*could come from difficulties! Thank You for showing*
*me how. In Jesus' name I pray. Amen.*

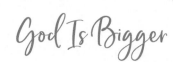

# God Is Bigger

*So I say to my soul, "Don't be discouraged. Don't be disturbed.*
*For I know my God will break through for me." Then I'll have*
*plenty of reasons to praise him all over again. Yes,*
*living before his face is my saving grace!*
PSALM 42:11 TPT

Everything earthly will fail us. We're imperfect people in community with other imperfect people all living in an imperfect world. That right there is a setup for discouragement. Marriages will end. Children will make wrong choices. Friends will betray. Loved ones will pass. Governments will have bad policies. Churches will mess up. And our bodies will wear out. But God will never fail us.

When life's circumstances hurt and people wound your heart, remind yourself that God is bigger than the struggles you're facing. Remember all the times He came through for you. Read scripture that encourages you to trust Him. And choose to believe that God is for you and working out the details for your good.

*Father, I'm trusting You for breakthrough.*
*In Jesus' name I pray. Amen.*

# Fear's Relationship to Punishment

*Love never brings fear, for fear is always related to punishment.*
*But love's perfection drives the fear of punishment far*
*from our hearts. Whoever walks constantly afraid of*
*punishment has not reached love's perfection.*

1 John 4:18 TPT

Take a deep breath, sweet one. Your heavenly Father isn't sitting on His throne just waiting for an opportunity to punish you. He isn't angry about something you did and looking for ways to make you pay. You don't disappoint Him, because God sees you through the sin-cleansing blood His Son spilled on the cross. There is no reason to fear Him because He's in love with you—His perfectly imperfect daughter.

The Lord is fully aware of your flaws. He knows every weakness and shortcoming. He's seen every mistake and failure. And God still says, *"I fully love you. I fully accept you. And I delight in you!"* Don't be afraid to be the wonderful you He created.

. . . . . . . . . . . . . . . . . . . . . . . . . . . . . . . . . . . . . .

*Father, help me walk in confidence of Your love rather than*
*in fear of Your punishment. In Jesus' name I pray. Amen.*

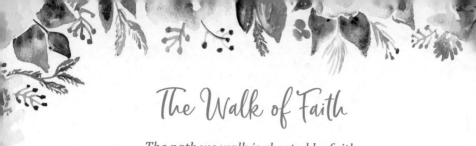

# The Walk of Faith

*The path we walk is charted by faith,*
*not by what we see with our eyes.*
2 Corinthians 5:7 voice

Rather than the situations we fear, the circumstances that make us insecure, the people who discourage us, or the struggles that feel too overwhelming, let's find courage to keep our eyes on *Jesus*. It's a choice that takes grit. This life requires us to trust Him way out of our comfort zone. Without fail, we must believe that God is who He says He is and that He will do what He says He will do.

Do you need that kind of faith? Are you desperate for the peace and comfort He can offer through the storms of life? Do you need to be fearless for what's ahead? Then friend, ask God for what you need, and He will give it to you.

. . . . . . . . . . . . . . . . . . . . . . . . . . . . . . . . . . . . .

*Father, I'm weary from staring at my struggles. They overwhelm my*
*heart. Would You make me brave enough to trust You with*
*my circumstances instead? In Jesus' name I pray. Amen.*

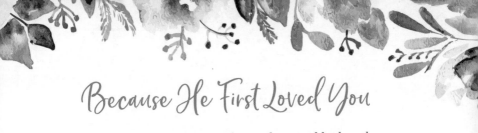

# Because He First Loved You

*We, though, are going to love—love and be loved.*
*First we were loved, now we love. He loved us first.*
1 JOHN 4:19 MSG

Even in our crunchy, messy, ugly, exhausting, drama-filled, overwhelming, imperfect moments, God loves us. While others may walk away out of frustration, God sticks with us. Always. He sees the good in us when others cannot. He knows the value we hold when others toss us aside. And the truth is, there's nothing we can do to make Him love us more or less than He does right now.

Because God first loved us, we've been shown what unconditional love looks like. This beautiful example is what teaches us how to be devoted to others. We cannot love as perfectly as He does, but we can learn to care for others with purpose.

*Father, I am so thankful for how well You love me. Your example*
*teaches me how I can treat others so they know how much*
*I care for them. In Jesus' name I pray. Amen.*

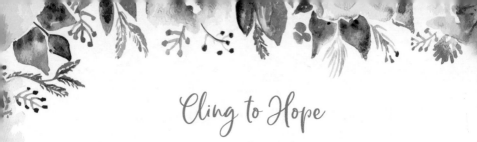

# Cling to Hope

*So now we must cling tightly to the hope that lives within us,*
*knowing that God always keeps his promises!*
Hebrews 10:23 TPT

Hope is a powerful motivator. It's why we get out of bed in the morning. It's why we muster the courage to try again. It's why we say yes when we want to say no. It's why we don't give in when the going gets tough. And the source of all hope is God. He is why we can freely hope for the desires of our hearts.

So what are you hoping for, sweet one? Maybe a new friend or a job that's more satisfying? Are you hoping for another opportunity to clear up a misunderstanding or the confidence to say what needs to be said? Maybe it's a restored relationship, someone special to marry, or a plus sign on your pregnancy test? Whatever it may be, cling to God. He is Hope.

*Father, I will place all my hope in Your promises!*
*In Jesus' name I pray. Amen.*

# God Is the Head of It All

*All that is great and powerful and glorious and victorious and
majestic is Yours, O Eternal One. Indeed everything that is in the
heavens and the earth belongs to You. The kingdom belongs
to You, O Eternal One, and You are the head of it all.*

1 CHRONICLES 29:11 VOICE

What an encouraging reminder that God is in control. He is in charge
of everything heavenly and earthly. He is the CEO of the universe and
rules over all existence. Nothing happens without His knowledge and
approval. Yep, God is the head of it all.

Here's why that's fantastic news. Since God is the One over all
things. . .we can rest. We can exhale. We can trust. This means we don't
have to figure it all out. We don't need to have all the answers because
He already does. So take a deep breath, grab a cup of coffee, and sit
back in your comfy chair. God's got this.

. . . . . . . . . . . . . . . . . . . . . . . . . . . . . . . . . . . . . . . . . . . .

*Father, thank You for having everything under control
so I don't have to! In Jesus' name I pray. Amen.*

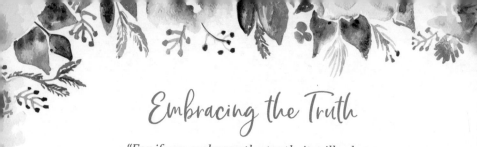

# Embracing the Truth

*"For if you embrace the truth, it will release*
*more freedom into your lives."*
JOHN 8:32 TPT

Choose to believe God's truths for your life. He's made power-packed promises designed to breathe life into your weary soul. And when you choose to take God at His Word, you'll find freedom. It will bring comfort and peace into your heart. And it will be a relief to know you're right where He wants you to be—in His loving care.

Maybe it's time to embrace this truth and be free. God made you special. He took His time to think you up. He didn't create you haphazardly but with great intention. And He designed a future for you to walk out—one filled with passion and purpose. God promises to walk that path with you daily, to give you all you need to live and love well. And He guarantees to work all things together for your good.

. . . . . . . . . . . . . . . . . . . . . . . . . . . . . . . . . . . . . . . . .

*Father, help me hold this truth close so I can live with*
*freedom to be me! In Jesus' name I pray. Amen.*

# He Makes Up the Difference

*So I'm not defeated by my weakness, but delighted! For when I feel my weakness and endure mistreatment—when I'm surrounded with troubles on every side and face persecution because of my love for Christ—I am made yet stronger. For my weakness becomes a portal to God's power.*
2 Corinthians 12:10 TPT

Can you remember being delighted by your weaknesses? Have you ever celebrated a failure? Have you faced defeat because of your limitations and been thrilled at the results? It's kind of laughable, really. God's way of seeing life is so very different from how the world sees it. Sometimes this concept feels too profound to understand. It's often counterintuitive and not relatable. But at the same time, there's a sense of comfort knowing that at the end of ourselves is a heavenly Father ready to make up the difference. He will always fill in the gaps that our human condition leaves exposed.

* * *

*Father, what a relief to know that when I get to the end of me, You're there. In Jesus' name I pray. Amen.*

# Always Listening

*GOD's there, listening for all who pray,*
*for all who pray and mean it.*
PSALM 145:18 MSG

God listens when you talk to Him, really listens. He's never distracted by someone else's problems. He doesn't run out of time to listen to your requests. God will never grow tired of hearing you ruminate over and over and over again about the same frustrations. And when you need someone to hear you out, He is always available.

So friend, talk away. Invite God into your heartache. Tell Him about all the things that are painful. Open up about who is driving you crazy and what you want to do about it. Rant and rave about situations out of your control. Lament about how someone hurt your feelings. Unpack the whole story with every detail spelled out. He's listening. What's more, all your secrets are safe with Him.

* * * * * * * * * * * * * * * * * * * * * * * * * * * * * * * * * * * * * *

*Father, thank You for being a safe place to share my heart. You are*
*such an awesome God, and I love You! In Jesus' name I pray. Amen.*

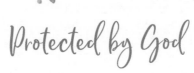

# Protected by God

*You're as real to me as bedrock beneath my feet, like a castle on a cliff, my forever firm fortress, my mountain of hiding, my pathway of escape, my tower of rescue where none can reach me. My secret strength and shield around me, you are salvation's ray of brightness shining on the hillside, always the champion of my cause.*

PSALM 18:2 TPT

Sit with this truth today, friend. Read it again. Repeat it out loud so your ears can hear it. Personalize it for yourself. Emphasize different words as you read out loud. Turn it into a song, singing it back to the Lord. Let this verse be your anthem.

There are few things that make us feel safe and secure in this world. Often, we're left to figure out issues on our own and fight battles we're ill-equipped to handle. So maybe God included this encouraging verse to remind us that we're forever protected by Him.

*Father, You are my Protector in every way. Thank You for loving me so well. In Jesus' name I pray. Amen.*

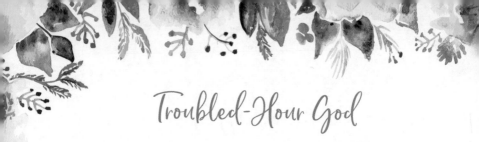

# Troubled-Hour God

*But me? I will sing of Your strength. I will awake with the sun to sing of Your loving mercy because in my most troubled hour, You defended me. You were my shelter.*

PSALM 59:16 VOICE

What does your troubled hour look like? Have you recently lost your job? Did the contract fall through? Are there more bills than money coming in? Is a parent facing a dire health report? Did your friend betray your trust? Was the secret exposed? Did you lose the house? Was the phone call jolting? We all will face troubled hours throughout life. But we don't have to do it alone.

This psalm is a beautiful reminder that God is a safe place for the brokenhearted. You can bring your mess right to Him. And He will be exactly who you need in that moment. He will protect, defend, heal, restore, encourage, affirm, or just listen. He is your troubled-hour God.

*Father, You are my safe place when no one else is. I love You. In Jesus' name I pray. Amen.*

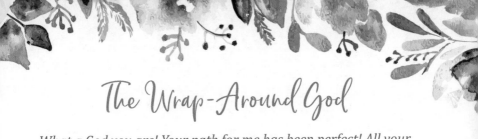

# The Wrap-Around God

*What a God you are! Your path for me has been perfect! All your promises have proven true. What a secure shelter for all those who turn to hide themselves in you! You are the wrap-around God giving grace to me.*
PSALM 18:30 TPT

The safest place to be when life spirals out of control is tucked away with Jesus. In the middle of chaotic times, we can find comfort by hiding ourselves in the Lord. He covers us fully and offers peace that makes no sense to the world.

How do you reach this refuge? You pray, asking for what you need. You listen to worship music with positive messages. You recite scripture that encourages your heart. You take negative thoughts captive and give them to God. You spend time reading His Word. Simply put, you're intentional to seek the wrap-around God who can handle your troubles.

* * * * * * * * * * * * * * * * * * * * * * * * * * * * * * * * * * * * *

*Father, I want to tuck away with You for shelter from the storms of life. I trust You to keep me safe. In Jesus' name I pray. Amen.*

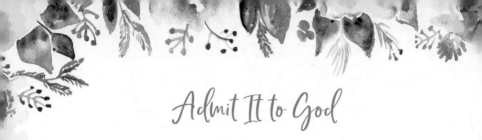

# Admit It to God

*I admit how broken I am in body and spirit,*
*but God is my strength, and He will be mine forever.*
PSALM 73:26 VOICE

Do you ever put on a brave face while inside you're falling apart? Do you smile when you want to break down and have an ugly-cry session? Sometimes it's hard to admit we're hurting because it feels too vulnerable. We're worried that others might judge us. So rather than be honest, we act like we're all put together.

The Lord wants you just as you are. He doesn't need you to act braver or stronger than you are in this moment. The ugly cry doesn't freak Him out, and He'll never label you as overdramatic. What's more, your Father wants to help you work through your feelings so He can heal your broken heart and restore your hope and joy.

. . . . . . . . . . . . . . . . . . . . . . . . . . . . . . . . . . . . . . . . . . . . .

*Father, I am broken. I admit I am overwhelmed and unable to handle this on my own. Will You please help me? In Jesus' name I pray. Amen.*

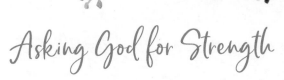

# Asking God for Strength

*Seek the Lord and His strength; yearn for and seek*
*His face and to be in His presence continually!*
1 CHRONICLES 16:11 AMPC

Scripture tells us we were created in God's likeness, but we were never given His god-ness. That is His alone. The Lord has supernatural abilities that are endless, while we're drastically limited by the human condition. God has everlasting power and might, but we will always get to the end of the rope. His strength is perfect and ours is anything but.

That's why we seek His strength rather than rely on our own. Without fail, we will eventually toy with giving in or giving up because the battle feels too big or too hard. We will look for shortcuts because we're exhausted. But if we humble ourselves and ask God to strengthen us, He will honor that request!

*Father, why do I always try to do everything by myself?*
*I know I need Your help to stay the course. I need Your strength.*
*And I am asking for that now. In Jesus' name I pray. Amen.*

# Craving a Resting Place

*He offers a resting place for me in his luxurious love.*
*His tracks take me to an oasis of peace, the quiet brook of bliss.*
PSALM 23:2 TPT

How our hearts crave rest. With everything we juggle as women, it's no wonder we're physically and emotionally exhausted. From managing the family calendar to meeting work demands to helping aging parents to getting dinner on the table, we need God's help to find peace in our busy lives.

What are the things you do in an effort to restore yourself? Exercise regularly? Read a good book? Spend time in nature? Meet friends for coffee dates? Schedule date nights? Make an appointment at a spa? While these pursuits are good, the kind of rest and peace you need can so often only be received by time with God. Make sure to invest in your relationship with Him.

*Father, I am running ragged and in need of the kind of rest and peace only You can provide. Will You help me? In Jesus' name I pray. Amen.*

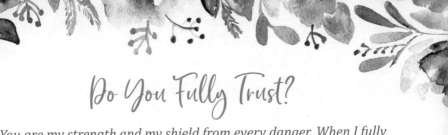

# Do You Fully Trust?

*You are my strength and my shield from every danger. When I fully trust in you, help is on the way. I jump for joy and burst forth with ecstatic, passionate praise! I will sing songs of what you mean to me!*

PSALM 28:7 TPT

When this truth becomes your truth, you can persevere through hard times. It's knowing that when you surrender to His strength, you'll have the courage to keep pressing forward to resolution. It's believing that God will provide you with the tools necessary to stand strong and battle with confidence. It's faith to take the next right step without hesitation because you know God will be right there with you. And it's radically trusting to be steadfast in your conviction that God is who He says He is and will do what He says He will do.

. . . . . . . . . . . . . . . . . . . . . . . . . . . . . . . . . . . . . . . . .

*Father, I am choosing to rely on Your Word and promises. I'm choosing to expect nothing less than Your faithfulness in my life. And I know Your help will always be available. In Jesus' name I pray. Amen.*

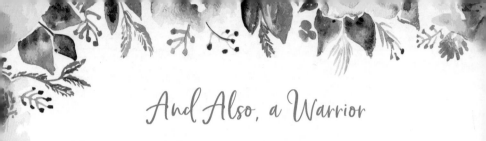

# And Also, a Warrior

*The LORD your God is in your midst—a warrior bringing victory.*
*He will create calm with his love; he will rejoice over you with singing.*
ZEPHANIAH 3:17 CEB

God has many names that accurately describe who He is to you. He is your Shield and Salvation. He's your Redeemer and Restorer. The Lord is Judge and Joy. He is Hope and Healer. God is the faithful, trustworthy, wise, mighty, all-knowing, omnipresent One and your Father in heaven. But He is also a Warrior.

We often decide that God is meek and mild, and we forget that He is also a powerful Protector of His children—one who brings victory every time. There are battles He asks you to fight, but there are other times He steps in and fights Himself. And when He does, a welcome calm settles over your heart because you know you are loved.

*Father, You are so many things to me. Today, I especially thank You for being a Warrior who protects me. In Jesus' name I pray. Amen.*

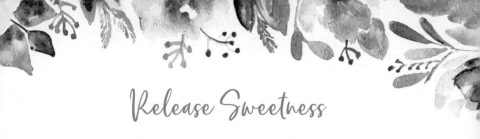

# Release Sweetness

*Nothing is more appealing than speaking beautiful,*
*life-giving words. For they release sweetness to*
*our souls and inner healing to our spirits.*
PROVERBS 16:24 TPT

Let your words be beautiful. Be mindful to speak life-giving expressions of love to those you care about. Use kindness when speaking to strangers. Let your speech be God directed because everyone needs to know they are worthy and valued. Well-placed words bring forth happiness.

Take a personal inventory of yours. How do you speak to your family? Is it encouraging? Are your words helpful? Do they build others up or do they tear them down? Do your words leave people in a better place or crush their spirits? In a world where you can be anything, choose to be kind.

*Father, I know what it feels like to have words used against me,*
*and I don't want to be reckless with mine. Will You give me wisdom*
*and discernment to know the right words to use at the right time?*
*And let my words always be life-giving. In Jesus' name I pray. Amen.*

# Full-Power Promises

*"Not one promise from God is empty of power,
for nothing is impossible with God!"*
LUKE 1:37 TPT

Do you ever make a promise knowing there's a good chance you won't be able to deliver? You may have every good intention to come through for someone, but there's still a twinge of doubt that it will happen. Or maybe you offer up empty promises because it's what you think someone needs to hear in the moment. This truth isn't pretty, but it's an honest reality for each of us at some point.

God's promises, on the other hand, are always fulfilled—every single one of them. If He says He will. . .He will. If the Lord reveals His plan or purpose, it will come to pass. What's more, God's promises never lose power or potency. He doesn't forget or forgo. His are the only vows that are 100 percent guaranteed to come into full bloom. So hold on to them, sweet one. They will be realized.

*Father, thank You for being true to Your Word.
In Jesus' name I pray. Amen.*

# An Inheritance of Protection

*"No weapon that is formed against you will succeed; and every tongue that rises against you in judgment you will condemn. This [peace, righteousness, security, and triumph over opposition] is the heritage of the servants of the LORD, and this is their vindication from Me," says the LORD.*

ISAIAH 54:17 AMP

We serve the Lord because of His goodness. We worship and praise Him because of His faithfulness. We share our testimony with the world because we know its power. We love God because He first loved us. And because we are His children, we receive an impressive inheritance of protection.

The Lord promises that no weapon used against you will defeat you. The Enemy's plans will fail. And everyone who sits in judgment and speaks out against you will be proven wrong. God won't allow anything to harm you. You'll have hard seasons of life, but He'll bring good from them. You will always rise up from the ashes.

• • • • • • • • • • • • • • • • • • • • • • • • • • • • • • • • • • • • • • • • • •

*Father, help me trust in Your protection. In Jesus' name I pray. Amen.*

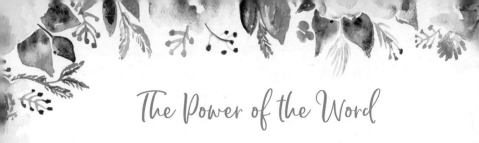

# The Power of the Word

*Every Scripture has been written by the Holy Spirit, the breath*
*of God. It will empower you by its instruction and correction,*
*giving you the strength to take the right direction and*
*lead you deeper into the path of godliness.*

2 TIMOTHY 3:16 TPT

The Word of God is relevant today. While it was written thousands of years ago, it's still applicable to your life. Men may have put pen to paper, but every word was God inspired and approved. Don't let anyone tell you differently.

God uses the Bible to reveal Himself. It's where He tells His story of faithfulness and love, and it's meant to help you live your best life. That's why it's vital you spend time in it on the regular. God's Word will teach you ways to embrace life to its fullest. It will show you how to make better choices. It details God's hope and expectation for living. And it will encourage you through tough seasons of life.

*Father, I'm so thankful for Your Holy Word!*
*In Jesus' name I pray. Amen.*

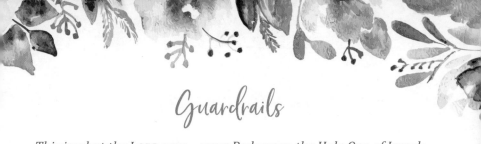

## Guardrails

*This is what the LORD says—your Redeemer, the Holy One of Israel:*
*"I am the LORD your God, who teaches you what is best for you,*
*who directs you in the way you should go."*
ISAIAH 48:17 NIV

God has a long history of teaching His children how to live right. From Adam and Eve to Abraham. . .to Moses. . .to the Israelites. . .to you, God is intentional to help us learn His ways so we can experience His goodness. Humanity may not have the best track record for obedience, but that never discourages the Father from His steady course of direction.

Be careful not to consider His commands as oppression. They most certainly are not. Instead, they are guardrails to keep you heading down the right road with Him. These guardrails keep you in the bounds of His favor, and they set you up for abundant blessings.

*Father, I know Your commands are for my benefit because You love me so much. Help me embrace them rather than be frustrated. In Jesus' name I pray. Amen.*

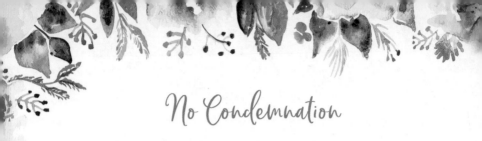

# No Condemnation

*No one who believes in Him has to fear condemnation,*
*yet condemnation is already the reality for everyone who refuses*
*to believe because they reject the name of the only Son of God.*
JOHN 3:18 VOICE

If you believe that Jesus is the Son of God and have invited Him into your life, you will not be judged as guilty. There will be no condemnation. But for those who don't believe, there will be a reckoning. Still, be careful you don't confuse condemnation with conviction.

Conviction is the Holy Spirit's job. It may be that gut check that makes you think twice when you're about to make a bad decision. It could be a sudden feeling—an intuition—that you need to rethink your choice and reconsider your next move. It's His still, small voice that whispers into your spirit, *"Don't do it."*

*Father, I believe in Your Son. I know Him to be Your one and only*
*Son. I'm grateful that step of faith keeps me from being*
*judged as guilty. In Jesus' name I pray. Amen.*

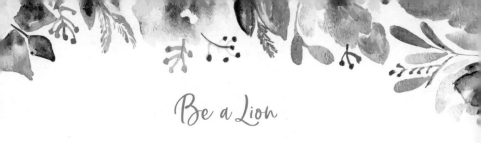

# Be a Lion

*The wicked are edgy with guilt, ready to run off even when no one's*
*after them; honest people are relaxed and confident, bold as lions.*

PROVERBS 28:1 MSG

When truth is on your side, you have nothing to fear. You know God is pleased, and that's what really matters. You should live your life caring more about embracing honesty than trying to hide your sins. This kind of resolve breeds confidence in who you are. And since there's no such thing as true perfection in our fallen humanity, it shouldn't be hard to embrace your messiness. It's okay to not be okay. Can't we just be honest about it?

What lies are you believing that make you unable or unwilling to share the reality of your situation? Whom are you trying to impress? Where are you feeling judged or condemned? Be encouraged that honesty isn't only the best policy, it also brings a calm confidence with it.

. . . . . . . . . . . . . . . . . . . . . . . . . . . . . . . . . . . . . . .

*Father, I don't want to hide my reality out of fear. Would You give*
*me courage to live authentically? In Jesus' name I pray. Amen.*

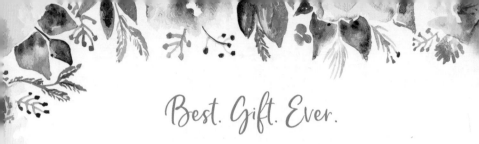

# Best. Gift. Ever.

*The payoff for a life of sin is death, but God is offering*
*us a free gift—eternal life through our Lord Jesus,*
*the Anointed One, the Liberating King.*

ROMANS 6:23 VOICE

Do you like to get gifts? Maybe it's one of the ways you feel loved. Maybe you are giddy on Christmas morning or at your birthday celebration, excited to see the thoughtful treasures others purchased or created for you. Well, think about this: as awesome as these offerings can be, they're nothing compared to the gift of eternal life—the gift of forever in heaven with the Lord. And when you invite Jesus to rule in your life, eternity is God's remarkable reward for your faith. His Son and your belief in Him worked together to create the overwhelming gift of heaven. Let's see if anyone can top that!

* * * * * * * * * * * * * * * * * * * * * * * * * * * * * * * * * * * * * *

*Father, never let me forget that You are the greatest gift giver of*
*all time. I'm so thankful You gave me the opportunity to spend*
*all of forever with You! In Jesus' name I pray. Amen.*

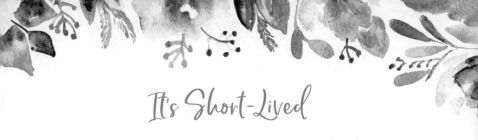

# It's Short-Lived

*We view our slight, short-lived troubles in the light of eternity.*
*We see our difficulties as the substance that produces for*
*us an eternal, weighty glory far beyond all comparison.*
2 CORINTHIANS 4:17 TPT

It could be a bent toward drama that makes us overemphasize troubles we face. It could be that the season of turmoil is long and hard, and we're overwhelmed. There are sucker punches to the gut that come out of nowhere and knock us down. And sometimes, we lose hope and crumble in defeat. Whichever it is for you, ask God for perspective.

The truth is that everything you're facing right now is nothing compared to the goodness you'll experience in heaven. This life with its struggles is a breath, and God will give you what you need to get to the other side. So hold on to hope, knowing eternity with Him is going to knock your socks off.

*Father, please give me Your perspective so I can see my present*
*situation in light of eternity. In Jesus' name I pray. Amen.*

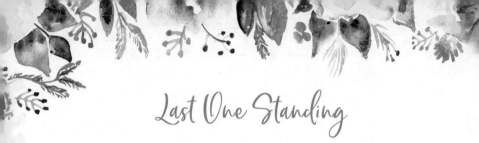

# Last One Standing

*For when I was desperate, overwhelmed, and about to give up,
you were the only one there to help. You gave me a way
of escape from the hidden traps of my enemies.*

PSALM 142:3 TPT

Who are your go-to people when life gets rough? Is it your mom or bestie? Is it a pastor, therapist, or spiritual mama? Think of the people who are there when you need help the most. What an awesome group of support!

But the psalmist knew that at the end of the day, God was all he really had. He knew God was his ever-present hope when others fell short. It's good for you to know this truth too. The Lord is available at any hour, has access to endless resources, can fill you with His strength and wisdom, and knows the entire situation from front to back. He will always be the last One standing next to you.

. . . . . . . . . . . . . . . . . . . . . . . . . . . . . . . . . . . . . . . . . .

*Father, others may love me well, but they can never outgive You.
I'm grateful. In Jesus' name I pray. Amen.*

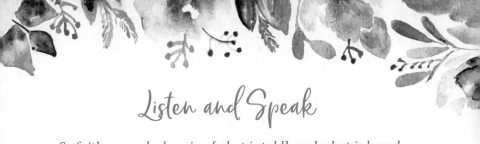

## Listen and Speak

*So faith comes by hearing [what is told], and what is heard comes by the preaching [of the message that came from the lips] of Christ (the Messiah Himself).*

ROMANS 10:17 AMPC

This verse reminds us that we're auditory learners. It's important that we listen to others as they share their testimony because it helps solidify the Truth in us. When we hear stories of how God intersected a broken life or how peace was ever present in a chaotic situation, we're reminded of how powerful the Lord is. And since He's done it once, our faith will strengthen that He will do it again.

In the same way, be a woman eager to share God's goodness in your life with others. People in your circle need encouragement that He will prove Himself faithful for them too. Your testimony can help bring hope and peace to someone who desperately needs it.

. . . . . . . . . . . . . . . . . . . . . . . . . . . . . . . . . . . . . . .

*Father, there is power in our stories. Help us listen and speak so we'll be reminded of Your greatness. In Jesus' name I pray. Amen.*

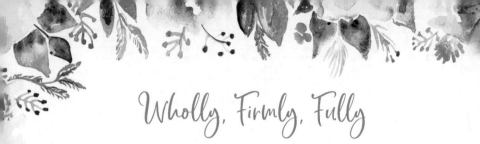

# Wholly, Firmly, Fully

*And whatever you ask for in prayer,*
*having faith and [really] believing, you will receive.*
MATTHEW 21:22 AMPC

God is asking for our full attention when we pray. Sometimes it's easy to let our minds wander to the item we should add to the grocery list, the phone call we need to return, the appointment we forgot to make, and the replaying of the fight we had the night before. We lose focus and fall into an almost robotic prayer time, struggling to connect to the Father. If we're not careful, our prayer life can become a half-hearted effort. And we'll eventually end up feeling frustrated and unheard.

But when our hearts are wholly engaged, when our minds are firmly on the Lord, when our desires align with His plan, and when our faith is fully activated, we will receive what we ask for. God says so.

*Father, thank You for being a God who answers prayers.*
*Help me wholly, firmly, and fully focus on You as I pray.*
*You deserve my complete attention. In Jesus' name I pray. Amen.*

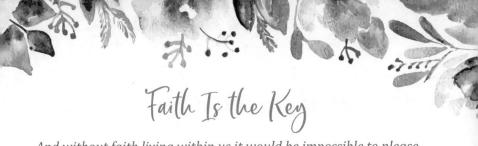

# Faith Is the Key

*And without faith living within us it would be impossible to please*
*God. For we come to God in faith knowing that he is real*
*and that he rewards the faith of those who give all*
*their passion and strength into seeking him.*
HEBREWS 11:6 TPT

Faith is the key that unlocks a beautiful relationship with God. If we choose not to believe in Him—or if we live a lukewarm existence, unwilling to go all-in with the Lord—it's not possible to please Him. Our wholehearted dedication to Him is a requirement. It's a nonnegotiable. And when we activate trust, it not only pleases God but also brings into bloom the realness of who He is and the faithfulness He offers those passionately seeking Him.

How about you? Are you zealous for the Lord, or is He your go-to only when you're in a pinch? Do you fervently seek a relationship with Him, or is He an afterthought?

. . . . . . . . . . . . . . . . . . . . . . . . . . . . . . . . . .

*Father, I'm choosing to be a faith-filled woman*
*who's all-in for You! In Jesus' name I pray. Amen.*

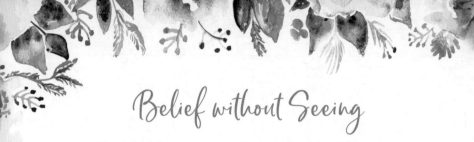

# Belief without Seeing

*Now faith brings our hopes into reality and becomes
the foundation needed to acquire the things we long for.
It is all the evidence required to prove what is still unseen.*
HEBREWS 11:1 TPT

The essence of faith means we choose to believe without having to see. It means we don't need to look into God's eyes to believe that He is real. Faith is choosing to be confident that God will come through even when the future looks grim. It means we decide to hold on to hope, being certain that the Lord is going to show up.

Every day, you're faced with opportunities to activate your faith. From struggles in your marriage, to heartache for your child, to losing a job, to a scary call from your doctor, you get to choose whether you trust God or give in to fears. Choose wisely, because faith says you can trust an unknown future to a known God.

· · · · · · · · · · · · · · · · · · · · · · · · · · · · · · · · · · · · ·

*Father, I don't need to see to believe in Your goodness!
In Jesus' name I pray. Amen.*

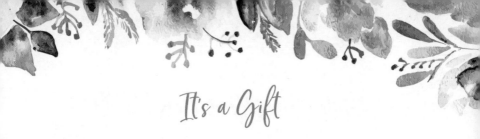

# It's a Gift

*For it's by God's grace that you have been saved. You receive it through faith. It was not our plan or our effort. It is God's gift, pure and simple. You didn't earn it, not one of us did, so don't go around bragging that you must have done something amazing.*
EPHESIANS 2:8–9 VOICE

Too often we fall into the trap of thinking it's our good works that get us to heaven. It can be hard to grasp that we'll be in eternity with God simply through faith alone. So in our confusion we try to make up the difference. We volunteer countless hours at school. . .we deliver food to the needy during the holidays. . .we financially support worthy causes with our paychecks. . .we stay busy doing everything we can to justify a ticket to heaven.

But sweet one, it's by God's grace that you've been saved. It's a gift, something you can never earn. Take a moment to share your appreciation with Him.

. . . . . . . . . . . . . . . . . . . . . . . . . . . . . . . . . . . . . .

*Father, thank You for the gift of salvation!*
*In Jesus' name I pray. Amen.*

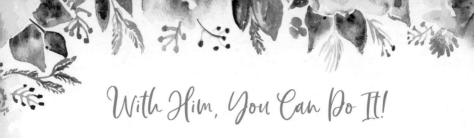

# With Him, You Can Do It!

*Whatever I have, wherever I am, I can make it through*
*anything in the One who makes me who I am.*
<small>Philippians 4:13 msg</small>

When people say you can do anything you put your mind to, that encouragement is not completely accurate. The truth is we all face limitations. God created us with different giftings and talents. A more precise statement would be "You can do all things with Jesus." He's the One who fills the gaps and makes up the difference. Without Jesus, we're severely limited by our human condition.

If your heart desires something, invite the Lord into it. Chances are He's the One who put the desire there to begin with. Ask Him to open the right doors or close ones you're not to walk through. Ask for an extra measure of faith and confirmation that you're on the right track. Talk with Him about any fears or insecurities and where you need His help.

*Father, I know with You I can do anything!*
*In Jesus' name I pray. Amen.*

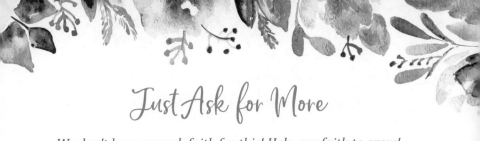

# Just Ask for More

*We don't have enough faith for this! Help our faith to grow!*
LUKE 17:5 VOICE

Have you asked God to increase your faith? He doesn't just admire your willingness to admit your need for Him; the Lord is ready to give you what you need! It's okay to admit you don't have enough faith for what's ahead. It's normal to feel ill-equipped to take the next step. There's no shame in being anxious about big changes you have to navigate. Confessing your weakness gives God room to be big in your difficult circumstances.

Where do you need more faith? Are monthly bills more than your monthly income? Did the mammogram show something of concern? Are you worried about your marriage? Are you about to take a new job that feels too big? We all need an extra dose of faith to walk out our lives. Just be honest with God and ask for more of it.

*Father, I feel so weak and worried about the next step.*
*Please increase my faith. In Jesus' name I pray. Amen.*

# Growing Your Faith Muscle

*He told them, "It was because of your lack of faith. I promise you,*
*if you have faith inside of you no bigger than the size of a small*
*mustard seed, you can say to this mountain, 'Move away from*
*here and go over there,' and you will see it move!*
*There is nothing you couldn't do!"*
MATTHEW 17:20 TPT

Can you remember the first time you went to the gym? You probably started lifting a small amount at first, gradually increasing weight and reps with each passing week. You were training your muscles to handle more. The goal was never to be an Olympic athlete; it was to have enough strength and tone to be healthy.

The Lord wants this for your faith. All you need is to believe in the power and might of God's ability. There's no room for doubt. If you can firm up your faith muscle to trust Him in all things, you will see results.

*Father, help me have the kind of faith that can*
*move mountains. In Jesus' name I pray. Amen.*

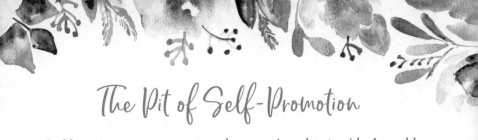

# The Pit of Self-Promotion

*God has given me grace to speak a warning about pride. I would ask each of you to be emptied of self-promotion and not create a false image of your importance. Instead, honestly assess your worth by using your God-given faith as the standard of measurement, and then you will see your true value with an appropriate self-esteem.*

ROMANS 12:3 TPT

Can we just be honest? Social media can be a self-promotion pit—a pit where we brag about our lives with false humility. We put our best moments online for all to see, with the goal of looking like we have it all together. And based on likes and comments from others, it's how we're gauging our worth.

God wants you to see your worth from His perspective. He wants you to know your value through His eyes. Because God created you with purpose, you delight Him. From your challenges to your celebrations, you are fully loved and accepted.

* * * * * * * * * * * * * * * * * * * * * * * * * * * * * * * * * * * * *

*Father, help me look for worth only from You.*
*In Jesus' name I pray. Amen.*

# Keep On Keeping On

*I have fought the good fight, I have stayed on course and finished the race, and through it all, I have kept believing.*
2 TIMOTHY 4:7 VOICE

You're not a quitter. It's not in your divinely designed DNA. You are a fighter, ready and able to face anything that comes your way. And when you ask the Lord to infuse you with His strength, wisdom, and perseverance, you're unstoppable.

Wanting to give up is a normal response to tough times. We all want to give in when the battle is long and overwhelming. But if God allowed this battle to come into your life, it's for your benefit and His glory. It's not for naught. And that means there's something in it that He wants specifically for you. So, trust God's reasoning. Seek His peace and comfort. And ask for endurance, because walking away can't be an option.

*Father, help me stay the course when I am weary.*
*I trust that there's something good in the journey and*
*beautiful at the finish line. In Jesus' name I pray. Amen.*

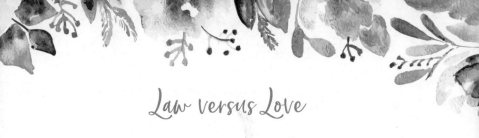

## Law versus Love

*But we know that no one is made right with God by meeting the demands of the law. It is only through the faithfulness of Jesus the Anointed that salvation is even possible. This is why we put faith in Jesus the Anointed: so we will be put right with God. It's His faithfulness—not works prescribed by the law—that puts us in right standing with God because no one will be acquitted and declared "right" for doing what the law demands.*

GALATIANS 2:16 VOICE

When Jesus died on the cross, it changed everything. No longer were we subscribed to the law, but instead we fell under the gift of grace. Love trumped law, and the blood of Jesus made us right with God. It cleansed us of sin in the eyes of the Father. Jesus was the ultimate atonement.

It wasn't anything we did that pleased God. Our works have no saving power. It was all Jesus.

*Father, my heart is full for what Jesus did for me on the cross. In His name I pray. Amen.*

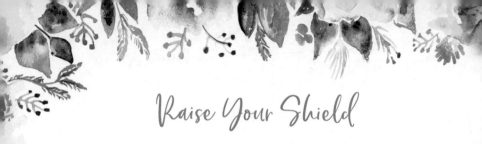

# Raise Your Shield

*Don't forget to raise the shield of faith above all else, so you will be
able to extinguish flaming spears hurled at you from the wicked one.*
EPHESIANS 6:16 VOICE

Do you know why God wants this for you? Because if you don't view
all the negatives in life through the lens of faith, you'll be left with an
overwhelming sense of hopelessness. Hurtful words, mean-spirited
actions, and joy-draining circumstances inevitably will be hurled in
your direction. No doubt you have firsthand knowledge of this. But
when you trust God—when you raise your shield of faith—the Enemy's
plans to knock you down fail.

It doesn't mean you won't feel sad or hurt. You are a human with
emotions. Instead, it means you know that God is bigger and that His
love for you will prevail. He is your protective Father. And when you
raise the shield of faith, you win.

*Father, help me raise my shield of faith to see every
circumstance through You. That's where my
strength lies! In Jesus' name I pray. Amen.*

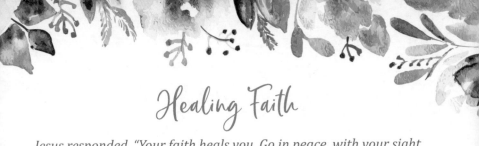

# Healing Faith

*Jesus responded, "Your faith heals you. Go in peace, with your sight restored." All at once, the man's eyes opened and he could see again, and he began at once to follow Jesus, walking down the road with him.*

MARK 10:52 TPT

The blind man chose to believe. He didn't know what clouds looked like or the colors in tapestries that hung throughout the city of Jericho. He had never been self-sufficient and instead relied on others for help. But he had a once-in-a-lifetime opportunity and he knew it. So when the Healer came his direction, he cried out to Jesus, who rewarded the man for his faith, giving him sight.

Where are you desperate for healing, friend? Is it your health, your finances, a relationship, or a debilitating fear? Have you cried out to the Lord, telling Him what you need? He loves you and wants to hear your heart. Share it today.

. . . . . . . . . . . . . . . . . . . . . . . . . . . . . . . . . . . . . . . . .

*Father, hear my cries for Your help and healing.*
*I am desperate for You today! In Jesus' name I pray. Amen.*

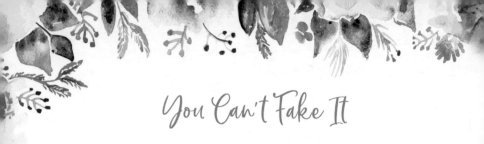

# You Can't Fake It

*So then faith that doesn't involve action is phony.*
JAMES 2:17 TPT

If someone says they are a lover of Jesus but are as mean as a snake, it's hard to believe their claim. If they say they follow the Lord's commands but make life choices in the opposite direction, their words and actions don't align. The truth is that if someone says they're a Jesus follower, their life should reflect His transformative power. There should be evidence of their commitment.

This isn't something you have to fake. When you accept Jesus as your Savior, the Holy Spirit lives within you and guides your decisions. You won't live a perfect life, but you will live one with purpose and passion. And as you grow in your relationship with God, your way of living and loving will preach a message of faith to those who know you.

· · · · · · · · · · · · · · · · · · · · · · · · · · · · · · · · · · · · · · · ·

*Father, I want my words and actions to reveal my faith in You. Help me be sensitive to the Holy Spirit's leading. In Jesus' name I pray. Amen.*

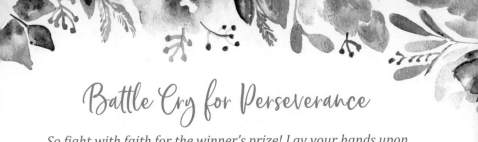

# Battle Cry for Perseverance

*So fight with faith for the winner's prize! Lay your hands upon eternal life, for this is your calling—celebrating in faith before the multitude of witnesses!*

1 TIMOTHY 6:12 TPT

This verse is a battle cry for persevering in your devotion to and trust in the Lord. Timothy encouraged believers to keep their faith no matter what disappointments and discouragements come their way. The reality is that life's burdens can wear you out and make you want to quit, but quitting goes against your dedication to God. You were chosen, called to have a life full of faith, and the hope is that you'll choose it no matter what.

Stand up, mighty warrior. You are a strong woman of God and capable of all things with His help. Cling to Him in this life, for doing so is a precursor to the beauty of your eternity in heaven.

. . . . . . . . . . . . . . . . . . . . . . . . . . . . . . . . . .

*Father, please give me strength to persevere in my faith.*
*I can endure anything with You. In Jesus' name I pray. Amen.*

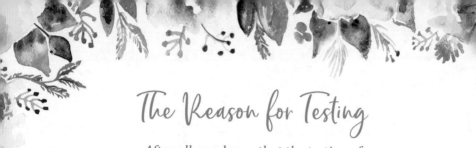

# The Reason for Testing

*After all, you know that the testing of*
*your faith produces endurance.*
JAMES 1:3 CEB

In this life you will have troubles. You may have already had enough to believe that statement without issue, but many think that being a Christ follower means you should be protected from harm. Wouldn't that be amazing? But that's not how faith works. We need the trials of life to help us be more like Christ. It's how we learn to be strong and courageous. It's how we learn to make the right decisions that are often the hard decisions. It's how our trust in God grows. And it's how we develop endurance for seasons of suffering.

Be careful not to resent God for allowing hard times in your life. He promises to be with you through it all, giving you everything necessary to be victorious.

*Father, help me change my perspective so I don't become angry*
*at You for the troubles I'm going to face. Instead, help me*
*trust You through them. In Jesus' name I pray. Amen.*

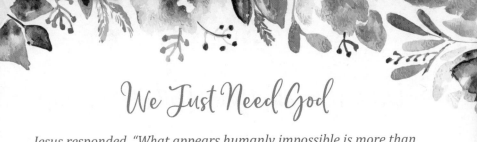

# We Just Need God

*Jesus responded, "What appears humanly impossible is more than possible with God. For God can do what man cannot."*
LUKE 18:27 TPT

Sometimes we feel like failures because we struggle in life. We want to love that pesky neighbor, but we can't seem to find the ability. We'd like to forgive our loved one for betraying our trust, but our minds keep replaying the offense. We feel like we should volunteer in our community or help with the church event, but we feel stingy with our time, so we don't. Left to our own devices, we can't muster the get-up-and-go attitude needed to live well and love others with care. That's why we need God.

All of these things are doable with Him. We can love, forgive, and be generous with our time when we ask for God's help. In His awesomeness, He can make anything possible.

. . . . . . . . . . . . . . . . . . . . . . . . . . . . . . . . . . . . . . . . . . .

*Father, thank You! I'm so limited in my humanness, but I'm grateful that with You I can be the kind of person who reflects You. In Jesus' name I pray. Amen.*

# Dear Woman, Your Faith Is Strong

*Then Jesus answered her, "Dear woman, your faith is strong!*
*What you desire will be done for you." And at that very moment,*
*her daughter was instantly set free from demonic torment.*

MATTHEW 15:28 TPT

Let this be your life's anthem! Let this be fuel that gets you pumped in the morning and allows you to sleep deeply at night. Let this be why you get right back up when the storms of life knock you down. Choose to be full of faith, deciding what God says is true and right. Because at the end of life, as you stand in front of your Creator, wouldn't it be humbling to hear the Lord say to you, "Dear woman, your faith is strong"?

So live passionately, trusting His perfect plan for your life. Never doubt He's working all things for your good. And believe with all your heart that the Lord's hands are deeply entrenched in your life, protecting and caring for you always.

. . . . . . . . . . . . . . . . . . . . . . . . . . . . . . . . . . . . . . .

*Father, help me have strong faith! In Jesus' name I pray. Amen.*

# He'll Keep You On Track

*Trust GOD from the bottom of your heart; don't try to figure out everything on your own. Listen for GOD's voice in everything you do, everywhere you go; he's the one who will keep you on track.*

PROVERBS 3:5–6 MSG

The Lord is the great Course Corrector. When He sees you heading down the wrong track, He will change your path. The Holy Spirit will give you those gut-check moments if you're making the wrong turn in life. When you're wandering aimlessly and feeling lost, God will illuminate the way. But you have to be seeking and listening for His direction.

Have you ever wished God would place big, bright billboard signs in front of you with arrows pointing where you're supposed to go next? It's often confusing to know the next right step. So be intentional to ask for His help and listen for His voice.

*Father, I trust You will direct my steps. Please give me ears to hear Your voice and I will follow. In Jesus' name I pray. Amen.*

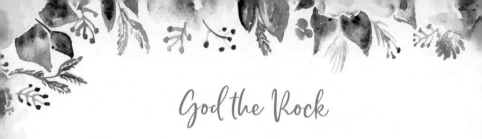

# God the Rock

*So trust in the Eternal One forever, for He is like a great
Rock—strong, stable, trustworthy, and lasting.*
ISAIAH 26:4 VOICE

Even with every good intention, friends and family will let you down sometimes. How could they not? We are imperfect people, living in an imperfect world, trying to love other imperfect people. And we have to have grace for them, because we are one of them. Amen? We try to be the rock others need, but we simply don't have the ability to be someone else's savior.

But God makes a whopper of a promise to us. He says He'll never let us down because He's like a great, massive rock. His strength to hold is unmatched. He is stable and unmovable. God is lasting and will always be here for us. And it's because of these steadfast truths that we can confidently believe God is forever trustworthy.

*Father, thank You for the visual of You being like a great Rock. It helps me better understand Your dependability. In Jesus' name I pray. Amen.*

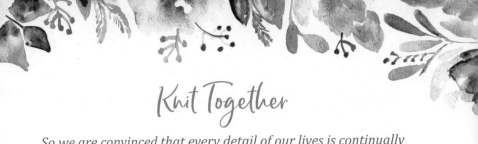

# Knit Together

*So we are convinced that every detail of our lives is continually
woven together to fit into God's perfect plan of bringing good
into our lives, for we are his lovers who have been
called to fulfill his designed purpose.*

ROMANS 8:28 TPT

This verse offers us powerful and much-needed encouragement! This is why we can endure those hard seasons without giving in to hopelessness. This is the reason we can find rest and peace and comfort in the Lord. This is the exact reason we don't give in or allow our hearts to become hardened with bitterness. Friend, this is good news.

God skillfully knits together the details of our lives—the awesome and the not so awesome—so they make sense. In the end, even the tough times are recognized as good and necessary. We don't know how He does it, but He does it just the same. Oh how He loves us.

. . . . . . . . . . . . . . . . . . . . . . . . . . . . . . . . . . . . . . . . . . .

*Father, I'm grateful You make all things new and good. Help me see
Your gift of goodness prevail. In Jesus' name I pray. Amen.*

# He Knows Everything about You

*In the beginning, God created everything:*
*the heavens above and the earth below.*
GENESIS 1:1 VOICE

God has always been. Isn't that hard to wrap your mind around? He wasn't created; He just was. He is. And the beginning of everything started with Him. Our Father thought up the heavens and the earth and all things that would inhabit them both. He separated the waters and the land and decorated them with life. The Word of God starts with this powerful verse for a good reason.

Knowing that God is a constant force reminds us that He never changes. He doesn't wear down. And what's more, He's involved in the details of life. God knows the ins and outs of creation, which means He has a thorough understanding of you. When you need clarity in a situation, talk to God. When you are struggling to understand a feeling, ask Him for insight. Your God knows everything about you.

* * * * * * * * * * * * * * * * * * * * * * * * * * * * * * * * * * * * * *

*Father, I'm comforted knowing You have comprehensive*
*knowledge of every single thing. In Jesus' name I pray. Amen.*

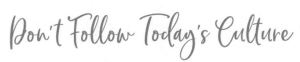

# Don't Follow Today's Culture

*Stop imitating the ideals and opinions of the culture around you,
but be inwardly transformed by the Holy Spirit through a total
reformation of how you think. This will empower you to
discern God's will as you live a beautiful life,
satisfying and perfect in his eyes.*

ROMANS 12:2 TPT

Can we agree there's pressure to fit in? We want to be liked, and that usually means we compromise what we know is *right* for what we know will help us be *accepted*. So we spend money we don't have to keep up with the Joneses. We make choices that lead us down the wrong paths morally. We focus our time on worldly pursuits more than deepening our relationship with God. And we care more about what others think of us than living a faith-filled life.

Ask the Lord to transform your thinking so culture no longer drives you. Ask for discernment to know the righteous ways of living.

. . . . . . . . . . . . . . . . . . . . . . . . . . . . . . . . . .

*Father, help me care more about what You think than
what the world thinks. In Jesus' name I pray. Amen.*

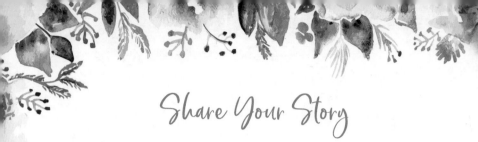

# Share Your Story

*"Therefore, go and make disciples of all nations, baptizing them in the name of the Father and of the Son and of the Holy Spirit."*

MATTHEW 28:19 CEB

Part of your God-designed purpose on earth is to spread the Good News of Jesus through your life. Never pass up an opportunity to encourage someone with your own story of God's faithfulness, because your testimony is more powerful than you realize. Others need to know there is hope in their own situation. When you tell your story of restoration, it allows the Lord to bolster endurance and courage in another. Your story of God's faithfulness to intervene at the right moment offers others confidence to believe He will for them too.

And when you're intentional to point out God's work in your own life, it helps to bring others into a relationship with Him. Your story becomes the encouragement someone needs to accept Jesus' gift of salvation and find comfort for their soul.

* * * * * * * * * * * * * * * * * * * * * * * * * * * * * * * * * * *

*Father, I will share my testimony with anyone who will listen! In Jesus' name I pray. Amen.*

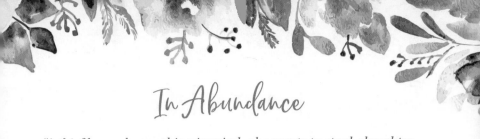

# In Abundance

*"A thief has only one thing in mind—he wants to steal, slaughter, and destroy. But I have come to give you everything in abundance, more than you expect—life in its fullness until you overflow!"*
<small>John 10:10 TPT</small>

There's a thief whose only goal is to discourage and destroy you. He walks the perimeter of your life, looking for any way in so he can wreak havoc. At every turn, he brings temptation in hopes that you'll choose sin. He brings destruction to your relationships expecting you'll become bitter. The devil is real, and he only has one thing on his mind—your demise.

But have hope! Jesus trumped the Enemy. That doesn't mean you won't have hard seasons to endure. That's just part of life on earth. But it does mean those hard seasons don't have to beat you. When you trust your life to God and lean on Him during tough times, you will receive everything you need in abundance to rise victoriously.

* * * * * * * * * * * * * * * * * * * * * * * * * * * * * * * * * * * *

*Father, my trust is in You! In Jesus' name I pray. Amen.*

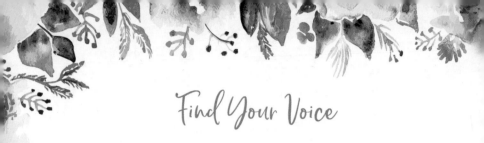

# Find Your Voice

*One night the Lord said to Paul in a vision,*
*"Don't be afraid. Continue speaking. Don't be silent."*
ACTS 18:9 CEB

God created you with a voice, and He wants you to use it. Too often we think we're to be meek and mild, quiet and complacent. We think our voice doesn't matter, that our opinions are better kept to ourselves. Rather than be bold and stand up for ourselves, we cower and stay silent. We endure hurt and harm rather than advocate for our needs. That's not God's plan for you, friend. You don't have to be afraid to speak up or speak out, because the Lord created your voice for a reason.

What you think matters. What you need matters. And what you have to say is important. While you have to be wise with your words and not use them as weapons, be ready to use them with passion and purpose. Find your voice.

. . . . . . . . . . . . . . . . . . . . . . . . . . . . . . . . . . . . . . . .

*Father, thank You for the gift of my voice and the*
*encouragement to use it! In Jesus' name I pray. Amen.*

# Something Miraculous Happened

*"My old identity has been co-crucified with Messiah and no longer lives; for the nails of his cross crucified me with him. And now the essence of this new life is no longer mine, for the Anointed One lives his life through me—we live in union as one! My new life is empowered by the faith of the Son of God who loves me so much that he gave himself for me, and dispenses his life into mine!"*

GALATIANS 2:20 TPT

When you said yes to Jesus, something miraculous happened. Your sins were forgiven and erased. Your old ways of living were replaced by Him living in you. His Holy Spirit took up residency in your heart, giving you the ability to live with righteous intention rather than only to please yourself. You now have power to point others to God with your words and actions. You have the ability to let your life preach of His goodness and faithfulness. Friend, let it be so.

* * * * * * * * * * * * * * * * * * * * * * * * * * * * * * * * * * * * * * * * * *

*Father, I will always say yes to You! In Jesus' name I pray. Amen.*

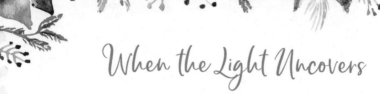

# When the Light Uncovers

*But if we freely admit our sins when his light uncovers them,*
*he will be faithful to forgive us every time. God is just to forgive*
*us our sins because of Christ, and he will continue to*
*cleanse us from all unrighteousness.*

1 John 1:9 TPT

When God's Holy Spirit in you brings sin to light, be quick to confess it. Right then and there, acknowledge your wrongdoing and ask for forgiveness knowing He will never hold it against you because of Jesus' work on the cross. He isn't expecting you to live a perfect life free of bad choices, but God knows that any sin kept in the dark can fester. The Enemy can use it against you, bringing shame and guilt that will eat you alive. So freely admitting your transgressions keeps you living in the full freedom that's yours thanks to the loving gift of Jesus.

. . . . . . . . . . . . . . . . . . . . . . . . . . . . . . . . . . . . . . .

*Father, help me be quick to confess my sins. I don't want the Enemy*
*to have any stronghold in my life. In Jesus' name I pray. Amen.*

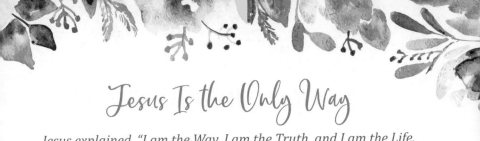

# Jesus Is the Only Way

*Jesus explained, "I am the Way, I am the Truth, and I am the Life.*
*No one comes next to the Father except through union*
*with me. To know me is to know my Father too."*

JOHN 14:6 TPT

There's only one way to secure your eternity in heaven with God. The Word says the road and the gate are narrow, but the world says otherwise. It spouts countless ways to God. Some think it's by good deeds, working yourself to the bone to be good enough. Some think it's following specific rituals and the letter of the law. Some believe eternity is possible by choosing to love everyone. And the list goes on.

But the Bible is clear when it says the only way to the Father is to believe that Jesus is His Son and accept His transformational gift of forgiveness. Rest in this truth today.

*Father, I know Your Son is the Way and the Truth and the Life.*
*My faith is anchored in Him. In Jesus' name I pray. Amen.*

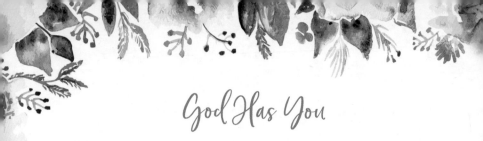

# God Has You

*This is My command: be strong and courageous. Never be afraid
or discouraged because I am your God, the Eternal One,
and I will remain with you wherever you go.*

JOSHUA 1:9 VOICE

If the all-powerful, all-knowing, ever-present God is for you, then who can possibly win any attack against you? Think about it. When God says you need to be strong and courageous, it's because you're backed by a mighty Father. When He tells you never to be afraid, it's because He'll fiercely protect you. And when God tells you not to give in to discouragement, it's because He is the lifter of your head.

What's more, He is with you always and wherever you go. Nothing about you or your circumstances escapes Him. So when you feel alone and afraid, take comfort in knowing that God has you.

*Father, it's so easy to get discouraged in life. There are so many
ways I feel weak and scared. Would You please bring peace
and encouragement to walk out this command?
In Jesus' name I pray. Amen.*

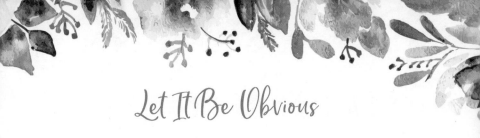

# Let It Be Obvious

*But give reverent honor in your hearts to the Anointed One and treat him as the holy Master of your lives. And if anyone asks about the hope living within you, always be ready to explain your faith.*
1 PETER 3:15 TPT

Every day, make the choice to honor God, recognizing Him as the holy Lord of your heart. Live in such a way that no one would question your devotion to Him. Make it obvious in the words you speak and in the ways you treat others that God is the most important relationship you have. And when people see there's something different about you and ask for an explanation, always be ready to open up about your faith in the Lord. Be prepared to tell them why you have hope, why you have peace. Be honest about why you don't live a defeated life of discouragement. Tell them about God.

. . . . . . . . . . . . . . . . . . . . . . . . . . . . . . . . . . . . .

*Father, I'm ready and willing to share You with whoever will listen. You're my hope and peace every day. In Jesus' name I pray. Amen.*

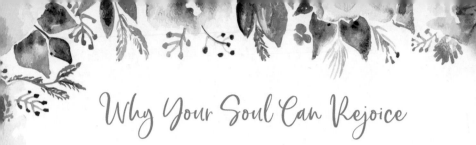

# Why Your Soul Can Rejoice

*We have become his poetry, a re-created people that will fulfill the destiny he has given each of us, for we are joined to Jesus, the Anointed One. Even before we were born, God planned in advance our destiny and the good works we would do to fulfill it!*

Ephesians 2:10 tpt

Like a beautifully strung together poem, you are God's masterpiece. With precision, He erased the old and remade you into something beautiful and powerful—a woman ready to live a life of purpose for the kingdom. It's the Lord who has made you who you are. And He is the One who planned in advance the good works destined for you to walk out in your one and only life on earth. His plan all along was for you to be a passionate lover of Jesus, living to glorify Him and point others to your Father in heaven. This is why your soul rejoices.

. . . . . . . . . . . . . . . . . . . . . . . . . . . . . . . . . . . . . . . . .

*Father, I'm made on purpose and for a purpose.*
*That's worth rejoicing about indeed! In Jesus' name I pray. Amen.*

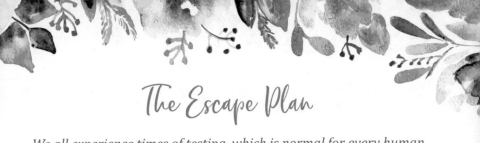

# The Escape Plan

*We all experience times of testing, which is normal for every human being. But God will be faithful to you. He will screen and filter the severity, nature, and timing of every test or trial you face so that you can bear it. And each test is an opportunity to trust him more, for along with every trial God has provided for you a way of escape that will bring you out of it victoriously.*

1 CORINTHIANS 10:13 TPT

What a gracious Father to ensure an escape plan for every trial you face—one that leads to victory in the end. The truth is that you will go through times of intense testing. It's just part of the human experience. But even in those times, God will always be faithful to know your limitations.

Trust that He screens and filters every test or trial so that you can survive it. And what's more, He'll meet your every need through it.

. . . . . . . . . . . . . . . . . . . . . . . . . . . . . . . . . . . . . . . . .

*Father, thank You for escape plans that lead to victory! In Jesus' name I pray. Amen.*

# His Presence Is Always Better

*Don't be obsessed with money but live content with what you have, for you always have God's presence. For hasn't he promised you, "I will never leave you alone, never! And I will not loosen my grip on your life!"*

HEBREWS 13:5 TPT

Money can buy you a lot, but it can't buy you time with the Lord. It won't help you develop a deeper relationship with Him. And you cannot purchase a ticket to eternity. Without fail, obsessing over money will leave you empty and always wanting more. Storing up worldly treasures doesn't benefit you in the end because you can't take them with you to heaven.

Make a decision to crave God's presence over worldly presents. It will be a huge step in the right direction to help you live a contented life because you'll be focused on the right things. It's key to a life of peace and plenty.

. . . . . . . . . . . . . . . . . . . . . . . . . . . . . . . . . . . . .

*Father, I know Your presence is always better than money. Help me live this truth. In Jesus' name I pray. Amen.*

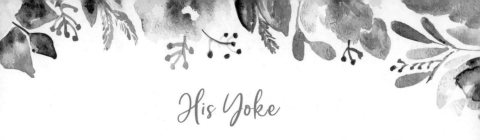

# His Yoke

*Put My yoke upon your shoulders—it might appear heavy at first,*
*but it is perfectly fitted to your curves. Learn from Me,*
*for I am gentle and humble of heart. When you are*
*yoked to Me, your weary souls will find rest.*

MATTHEW 11:29 VOICE

When the Lord says to put on His yoke, what He's asking is that you accept His plan for your life, that you walk it out with purpose, and that you learn from Him along the way. God acknowledges it may look crazy-scary because what He's asking is so far out of your comfort zone. He understands you might feel overwhelmed because it's not something you can do without His help and guidance.

But before you freak out, God is quick to remind us that He is gentle. He's not a slave driver. He's not expecting perfection or hours of overtime. Instead, if you choose to trust Him as you live out His plan, your weary soul will be restful and peaceful through it.

*Father, I'm all-in with You! In Jesus' name I pray. Amen.*

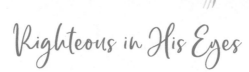

# Righteous in His Eyes

*For God made the only one who did not know sin to become sin for us, so that we who did not know righteousness might become the righteousness of God through our union with him.*

2 CORINTHIANS 5:21 TPT

Christ has no sin. He was completely pure and perfect and blameless. But God made Him step out of heaven, put on flesh, and take the place of our sin as He hung on the cross. He was the atonement for every sin you will ever commit, just as He was for everyone else too. Can you imagine the sacrifice?

This was God's demonstration of love. He loved you so much that He couldn't bear the thought of eternity without you. So rather than be separated from His prized creation and treasured possession, He sent Jesus to make all things right. He exhausted His wrath for sin on the cross, and now you're righteous in His eyes.

. . . . . . . . . . . . . . . . . . . . . . . . . . . . . . . . . . . . . . . . . . . . .

*Father, thank You for loving me so passionately that You sacrificed Your Son. In Jesus' name I pray. Amen.*

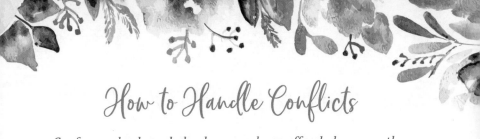

# How to Handle Conflicts

*Confess and acknowledge how you have offended one another
and then pray for one another to be instantly healed,
for tremendous power is released through the
passionate, heartfelt prayer of a godly believer!*

JAMES 5:16 TPT

Where are you struggling in your community of friends and family? Conflicts in marriage? Frustrations in a friendship? Warring with someone at work? Battles of the will with teenagers? Unrealistic expectations with parents? We can't always avoid fights with those around us.

But this verse offers the remedy for conflicts in relationships, and it promotes a powerful example for loving one another well. It may take guts and grit to walk out but promises a beautiful outcome. It starts with being humble and honest and ends with being passionate and prayerful. And it is good for the soul.

*Father, I admit this is hard for me! Give me the courage to be humble enough to see my offenses so I can confess them, and give me a willingness to forgive others' offenses too. In Jesus' name I pray. Amen.*

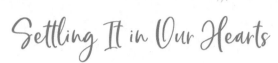

# Settling It in Our Hearts

*I am convinced that my God will fully satisfy every need you have,*
*for I have seen the abundant riches of glory revealed*
*to me through the Anointed One, Jesus Christ!*

<small>Philippians 4:19 tpt</small>

Have you seen God meet your needs? Has money shown up or a bill been anonymously paid? Did someone offer to help or a job open up at the right moment? Did the answer come in the nick of time or the health scare miraculously heal? These are the moments when we witness abundant riches of His glory in our circumstances.

It's important we settle His faithfulness in our hearts. We need to know without a doubt that God will come through again. We need this encouragement for us, but we also need to be able to convincingly share it with others who need hope too.

* * *

*Father, I remember the times You intervened in my life, and I will no longer doubt Your ability to be faithful. It's been settled in my heart once and for all. In Jesus' name I pray. Amen.*

# The Holy Spirit's Dwelling Place

*Or don't you know that your body is a temple of the Holy Spirit*
*who is in you? Don't you know that you have the Holy Spirit*
*from God, and you don't belong to yourselves?*
1 CORINTHIANS 6:19 CEB

Do you realize that when you accepted Jesus to be your personal Savior, a supernatural transaction took place? Your *yes* invited the Holy Spirit of God to live in you. In that beautiful moment, your body became His temple—His dwelling place. And He is the One who guides you as you navigate this life in faith. This means you no longer live for yourself. Instead, you're living for God and His purpose for your life.

So take care of your temple. Eat right, get good sleep, and exercise, but also be careful what you allow to infiltrate your mind and heart.

*Father, I'm so thankful for the Holy Spirit in my life. Help me*
*remember that my body is a temple so that I make choices*
*that reflect that belief. In Jesus' name I pray. Amen.*

# Loving out of Our Comfort Zone

*This is how we have discovered love's reality: Jesus sacrificed his life for us. Because of this great love, we should be willing to lay down our lives for one another.*

1 JOHN 3:16 TPT

Jesus gave up His throne to atone for the sins of the world. And as He hung on the cross—with legions of heavenly armies waiting for His signal, knowing He could at any moment access His own powers to stop the brutality—He saw your face in His mind's eye and chose you instead. Jesus loved you more than His comfort.

In the same vein, we should be willing to step out of our comfort zone to love others too. We may not be asked to die for another, but we will have opportunities to love when it's inconvenient. We can love those deemed unlovable. And with the Lord's help, we can find, as best as we can, the heart to love sacrificially.

* * * * * * * * * * * * * * * * * * * * * * * * * * * * * * * * * * * * * *

*Father, give me the courage to love others without conditions. In Jesus' name I pray. Amen.*

# Fostering an Atmosphere of Acceptance

*How wonderful, how beautiful, when brothers and sisters get along!*
PSALM 133:1 MSG

The world can be a hostile place. Today it seems like we're all living in offense, choosing sides in anger and vitriol. Too often we decide that if someone thinks differently than we do, we can't even be friends. Our society is so polarized, and our world feels like a time bomb waiting to explode.

You may not be able to change the world, but you can change how you love the community you've been given. You can model compassion and encourage others to accept differing opinions and ideas. You can foster an atmosphere of acceptance and tolerance. Doing this will not only benefit you but also glorify God in heaven. What's more, it will keep you in the peace of Jesus.

*Father, it breaks my heart to see so much hate in the world.*
*Sometimes I feel helpless. Would You guide me as I try to*
*create an atmosphere of love and acceptance within*
*my community? In Jesus' name I pray. Amen.*

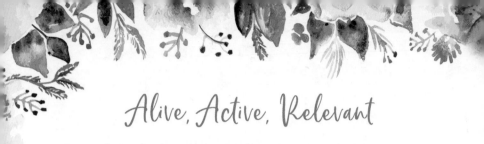

# Alive, Active, Relevant

*For we have the living Word of God, which is full of energy, and it pierces more sharply than a two-edged sword. It will even penetrate to the very core of our being where soul and spirit, bone and marrow meet! It interprets and reveals the true thoughts and secret motives of our hearts.*

Hebrews 4:12 TPT

The Word of God is alive, active, relevant, and full of energy. And it's sharp—sharper than a sword that's sharpened on both sides. It has the ability to cut right to the core of our souls and spirits, revealing truth in the darkest places of our hearts and minds. The Word instructs us on how to live. It uncovers hidden motives. It encourages our hearts. It convicts our sinful nature. It reminds us who God is and who we are. It's a powerful way that God reveals Himself to us. The Bible is a gift to be cherished.

. . . . . . . . . . . . . . . . . . . . . . . . . . . . . . . . . . . . . . . . . . .

*Father, thank You for the power of Your Word and how it's still relevant for me today. In Jesus' name I pray. Amen.*

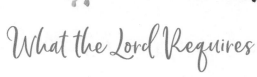

# What the Lord Requires

*He has told you, O man, what is good; and what does the LORD require
of you except to be just, and to love [and to diligently practice]
kindness (compassion), and to walk humbly with your God [setting
aside any overblown sense of importance or self-righteousness]?*
MICAH 6:8 AMP

This is the kind of verse that doesn't mince words. We can appreciate
the bluntness of God's command. He is sharing His expectations for His
followers and is asking us to care for others in three important ways.

We're to do what is right to others. We're to be conscientiously kind
and compassionate. And we're to be humble as we trust God, understanding our position in relation to His. How would your relationships
be changed for the better if you decided to follow these commands?
What would have to change to make this a reality? This life is but a
breath. Let's live it in peace with those we love.

. . . . . . . . . . . . . . . . . . . . . . . . . . . . . . . . . . . . . . .

*Father, help me be intentional to live and love according to
Your commands. In Jesus' name I pray. Amen.*

# Guard Your Time with Believers

*This is not the time to pull away and neglect meeting together,*
*as some have formed the habit of doing, because we need each*
*other! In fact, we should come together even more frequently,*
*eager to encourage and urge each other onward as*
*we anticipate that day dawning.*

HEBREWS 10:25 TPT

It's easy to get busy and neglect spending time with other believers. Be it your child's soccer practice, business dinners, date nights, work trips, volunteer hours, or family obligations, too often we allow our calendars to rule our lives. We forgo important things because we're tired or overwhelmed.

But it's important to guard your commitment to Sunday services, small groups, or Bible studies because you need the encouragement only they can offer—encouragement that's rooted in Christ. These are the friends who will rally around you in prayer. They will offer sound, biblical advice. And they will be the ones to remind you of God's power in your life.

* * * * * * * * * * * * * * * * * * * * * * * * * * * * * * * * * * * *

*Father, I understand the value of meeting together.*
*Help me keep it a priority. In Jesus' name I pray. Amen.*

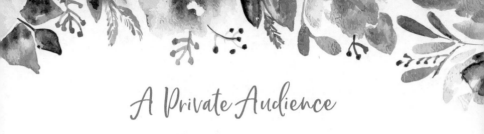

# A Private Audience

*So let us step boldly to the throne of grace, where we can*
*find mercy and grace to help when we need it most.*
HEBREWS 4:16 VOICE

You have complete freedom to come before the throne of God anytime you need to. You don't have to be in the right setting or muster up the right kind of words. There's no formula to follow or wrong way to talk to the Lord. Friend, when you bow your head to pray, you're supernaturally granted a private audience with the God who adores you.

In His presence there is grace. Loads of grace. And you will receive compassion, kindness, generosity, and understanding as you share with God what's on your heart. It's there you'll find comfort and peace for your soul. You'll find strength and wisdom. Actually, God is ready to equip you with all you need to take the next right step.

*Father, it means so much that I can come to You whenever*
*and wherever. I'm thankful for Your availability to*
*hear my heart. In Jesus' name I pray. Amen.*

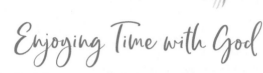

# Enjoying Time with God

*Make God the utmost delight and pleasure of your life,*
*and he will provide for you what you desire the most.*
PSALM 37:4 TPT

Do you enjoy the Lord? Does your time with Him delight you? As with any good relationship, you should cherish the times together. Whether you're sharing your day with Him, venting your frustrations, singing worship songs to Him with your hands held high, or digging into His Word, these times should be fulfilling. By the end, you should feel more loved and more valued. You should feel heard and seen. And you should be encouraged and confident in your next step. Time with God is never wasted time.

So find times every day to invite Him in. Let God walk out your day with you. Have fun together!

* * * * * * * * * * * * * * * * * * * * * * * * * * * * * * * * * * * * * * * *

*Father, I want You to be the highlight of my day. And I want to look forward to folding You into every moment. Thank You for wanting to spend time with me! In Jesus' name I pray. Amen.*

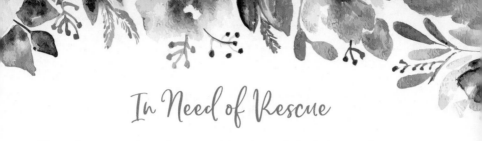

# In Need of Rescue

*There is no one else who can rescue us, and there is no other name under heaven given to any human by whom we may be rescued.*
ACTS 4:12 VOICE

When everything is falling apart, we naturally look for help. We look for someone who has answers we can't seem to find. We search for battle plans or escape routes so we don't have to face the giants before us. Because deep down, we feel ill-equipped. We decide the whole situation is above our pay grade. And we find ourselves desperate to be rescued.

But Jesus is there, waiting for you to ask for His help. He knows exactly what is needed to bring comfort and peace to your weary soul. He fully understands all your feelings. And Jesus has complete clarity of every detail. He is your hope—the only One who is able to save you.

*Father, I need Your help. I am in need of rescue.*
*And I am trusting that You will be everything I need*
*in this moment. In Jesus' name I pray. Amen.*

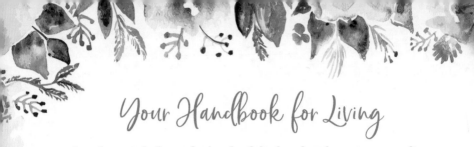

# Your Handbook for Living

*Let the words from the book of the law be always on your lips.
Meditate on them day and night so that you may be careful to live
by all that is written in it. If you do, as you make your way through
this world, you will prosper and always find success.*
JOSHUA 1:8 VOICE

The Bible is your handbook for living. There's nothing you'll ever face that isn't addressed in its pages. And the more time you spend reading and studying God's Word, the more equipped you'll be with wisdom and discernment. Let scripture be something you think about throughout your day, something you chew on with God. Share your thoughts with Him. Ask questions. Talk to your friends about it. And then be intentional to live out what you learn. Because if you do these things, you will find success in everything.

*Father, Your Word is such a gift. And I am committed to spending
time in its pages every day, learning godly ways of living and
choosing to live by them. In Jesus' name I pray. Amen.*

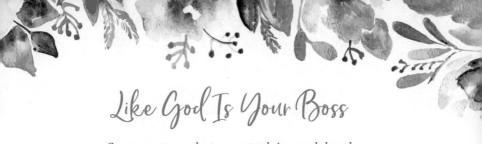

# Like God Is Your Boss

*So no matter what your task is, work hard.*
*Always do your best as the Lord's servant, not as man's.*
COLOSSIANS 3:23 VOICE

This verse is a call to be a hard worker full of integrity. It means being honest about the hours you're putting in. It means being truthful in your expense reports. It's a challenge to give your best to the job at hand, keeping a positive attitude.

Whether your job is running a company, organizing a big event, teaching in a classroom, leading yoga in a gym, selling insurance, volunteering at a shelter, writing for a magazine, or managing your family from home, work like God is your boss. This perspective will help you stay focused and joyful.

* * * * * * * * * * * * * * * * * * * * * * * * * * * * * * * * * *

*Father, looking at work from this angle will help keep me from feeling put out and frustrated. It will allow me to find joy and purpose in what I'm doing. And it will bring a sense of contentment to know I am serving You through it. In Jesus' name I pray. Amen.*

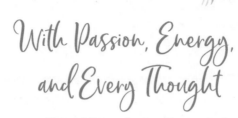

# With Passion, Energy, and Every Thought

*Jesus answered him, " 'Love the Lord your God with every passion of your heart, with all the energy of your being, and with every thought that is within you.' "*

MATTHEW 22:37 TPT

Jesus answered the question with simplicity. When the Pharisee asked Him what the greatest command was, the Lord was quick to respond. Of everything God asks of us, of all the commands documented in the Word, Jesus boldly said to love Him with all your heart, all your soul, and all your mind.

Friend, that's an all-in command. He wants the whole enchilada. The Lord doesn't want what you feel you can give in the moment. He doesn't want leftovers. No, He wants it *all*. Jesus wants your passion, energy, and thoughts. He wants to be all-consuming in your life because He's a jealous God. And going all-in will create peace inside you that's unmatched.

. . . . . . . . . . . . . . . . . . . . . . . . . . . . . . . . . . . .

*Father, I do love You. And I'm committing to love You with my passion, my energy, and my thoughts. I'm all-in! In Jesus' name I pray. Amen.*

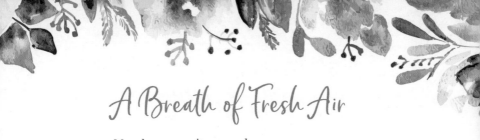

# A Breath of Fresh Air

*My plans aren't your plans, nor are your*
*ways my ways, says the LORD.*
ISAIAH 55:8 CEB

This truth is a blessing! What a breath of fresh air! We should be rejoicing to know that our plans are not like His. And we should be leaping for joy that His ways are not like ours. Think about it. How many relationships would you have demolished if He let you have your way? How many people would you have offended if left to your own devices? It is a good thing our God is smarter, more creative, and better able to discern right from wrong.

So where do you need His wisdom to prevail? Where do you need God to lead? In what situations do you need His clarity? Where do you need His perspective? Let God be the leader of your plans and ways. Follow Him so you'll stay in His peace.

. . . . . . . . . . . . . . . . . . . . . . . . . . . . . . . . . . . . . . . . . .

*Father, thank You that Your plans and ways are not*
*the same as mine! In Jesus' name I pray. Amen.*

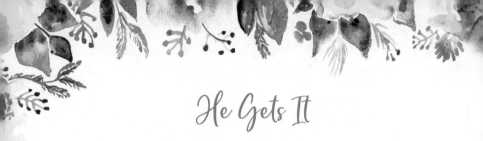

# He Gets It

*For Jesus is not some high priest who has no sympathy for our*
*weaknesses and flaws. He has already been tested in every way that*
*we are tested; but He emerged victorious, without failing God.*

HEBREWS 4:15 VOICE

Jesus can relate to anything you're struggling with. Because He came to the earth and fully experienced the human condition, there are no battles you will face that He can't understand. He gets it. He gets you. He knows how it feels to be weak against temptations. And Jesus can sympathize with your feelings of imperfection, failure, insecurity, and fear. He recognizes all the what-ifs and if-onlys that threaten to overwhelm you.

While on the earth, He was tempted in every way that we are tempted today, yet He didn't sin. And while that's not our story, it's good to know our God is able to empathize with us as we try to follow His lead and live a righteous life.

* * * * * * * * * * * * * * * * * * * * * * * * * * * * * * * * * * * * * * * * *

*Father, I'm so glad You can understand the trials and*
*temptations I face. In Jesus' name I pray. Amen.*

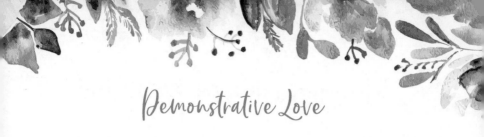

## Demonstrative Love

*"For when you demonstrate the same love I have for you by loving one another, everyone will know that you're my true followers."*
JOHN 13:35 TPT

Actions always speak louder than words. You may tell someone how much you value time with them, but when they rarely make it onto your calendar, the messages they receive don't jive. Maybe you offer to help a friend work through a tough time but are never available when they need a listening ear. But when you demonstrate your love for others, with your words and deeds lining up, they will experience the love of Jesus.

Because God loved you first, you have the ability to pass it on with great passion. The way you care for people, the selfless way you meet their needs, the kindness and compassion you spend on them will do something beautiful. They will know the Lord loves them.

*Father, I want to emulate Jesus, loving others in big ways.*
*Help me walk that out every day! In Jesus' name I pray. Amen.*

# More Inspiration for Your Soul

   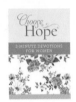

### *Choose Joy: 3-Minute Devotions for Women*
978-1-63409-998-1

### *Choose Prayer: 3-Minute Devotions for Women*
978-1-68322-398-6

### *Choose Grace: 3-Minute Devotions for Women*
978-1-68322-255-2

### *Choose Hope: 3-Minute Devotions for Women*
978-1-68322-174-6

Got 3 minutes to spare? You'll find the spiritual pick-me-up you crave in these inspiring 3-minute devotionals. Written especially for the twenty-first-century woman, these delightful books pack a powerful dose of comfort, encouragement, and hope into just-right-sized readings. Minute 1: scripture to meditate on; Minute 2: a short devotional reading; Minute 3: a prayer to jump-start a conversation with God.

Paperback / $4.99 each